ART AND ARTISTS IN CONNECTICUT

Library of American Art

ART AND ARTISTS IN CONNECTICUT

By H. W. French

Kennedy Graphics, Inc. • *Da Capo Press*
New York • *1970*

This edition of *Art and Artists in Connecticut*
is an unabridged republication of the first edition published
in Boston and New York in 1879.

Library of Congress Catalog Card Number 70-87543
SBN 306-71459-0

Published by Kennedy Graphics, Inc.
A Division of Kennedy Galleries, Inc.
20 East 56th Street, New York, N.Y. 10022

and

Da Capo Press
A Division of Plenum Publishing Corporation
227 West 17th Street, New York, N.Y. 10011

Manufactured in the United States of America

ART AND ARTISTS IN CONNECTICUT

COL. JOHN TRUMBULL. FROM THE MARBLE BUST
IN THE YALE ART GALLERY.

THE PIONEERS OF ART IN AMERICA.

ART

AND

ARTISTS IN CONNECTICUT.

BY

H. W. FRENCH.

BOSTON:
LEE AND SHEPARD, PUBLISHERS.
NEW YORK:
CHARLES T. DILLINGHAM.
1879.

Dedication.

THERE is a custom, a very good and appropriate custom, of honoring heroes with laudations of one kind or another, that shall to some extent indicate their noble deeds. Certain considerations entitle Connecticut to the position of a heroine among her sister States. As such this tribute is offered, in the belief that a record of her art-life will be to her glory; and is respectfully dedicated to the people of the State.

INTRODUCTION.

THE history of the fine arts in a single State, at first thought, would appear either thoroughly insignificant, or so closely allied to the art-life of other States as to be of no interest if isolated and prepared without reference to those others. Nevertheless, the more careful the study bestowed upon the subject, the more evident it will become that there may be exceptions. One intimate with the history of the fine arts in Connecticut will be readily convinced that this State presents, to the lover of art, a romance richly meriting an individual chronicle.

The subject is one which has been much neglected throughout the States, even by those who derive the most benefit and pleasure from the productions of art. This lack of interest is due in great part to ignorance and prejudice, which the good public will gladly do away with if it may be made apparent, together with a means of relief. We take a national pride in the perfection of that which comes in competition with the productions of Europe. Strangely, in the arts of painting and sculpture, that most of all display the direct power of man's mind and hand, there is less interest and enthusiasm on the part of the public than in any other production. Doubtless art depends upon justice for success. But the public is not always just. Not that it is in the heart of man to abuse willingly, but that unintentionally many hinderances are placed in the way of art-progress, and much injustice done. The most comprehensive view of a landscape, a day, or a lifetime, is a retrospective view.

If the signs of the times be true, that the love of art is waxing strong in the States, a glance backward, before too many steps are taken, may be of great value in securing a progress which shall be warned by the failures of the past, advised by the experiments, encouraged and directed by the successes. We can more easily recognize and denounce injustice and prejudice when we see them in history than when they become a part of daily life and common custom. Cause and effect are then more clearly defined in their relationship. Just now is a time of unusual enthusiasm, a season of art-revival, such as in former days preluded the advent of men like Apelles and Angelo. There will be grand results in the United States outgrowing from this; and that State to set herself most systematically and emphatically to the task of taking the tide at its full flood will be the first to be led on to fortune.

A local history of art, which, as in the case of Connecticut, covers but little over a century, cannot well be more or less than a biographical record of artists who have borne their part. Upon this conclusion such sketches have been carefully prepared. A few important facts are culled from former publications ; but it has been possible to gather many personal recollections concerning almost every artist, and the greater part of each history given hereafter will be formed from entirely new matter. Every living artist has been consulted, either personally or by letter ; the former being the case with a very large majority. If any thing in the coming papers shall prove of value, it is due to the fact that hardly an artist who has been consulted has expressed an unwillingness to assist in the preparation of the work ; and, without exception, those whose names do most honor the history of art in Connecticut have been in equal ratio most ready to facilitate the collection of information. In a great variety of ways, from the abundant resources thrown open by artists and their friends, the facts, criticisms, and details have been obtained.

To make a complete history of the art, it has appeared that others than simply natives of the State should be included, — such, for instance, as, having identified themselves with the State, either by long residence, by holding important positions as instructors in art, or by having produced in the State pictures of pre-eminent merit, have obviously imparted an important influence.

While, among the practitioners in the arts of design, architects and engravers are as justly included as sculptors and painters, the large number of the latter two must exclude for the present the former : although, of the former, engravers do most emphatically belong to Connecticut ; for in the history they form such an important part, that, instead of neglect, they demand especial and individual attention. This they shall receive in a more appropriate manner hereafter. For the present, painters and sculptors alone form the topic of investigation.

Among other difficulties, a great one has appeared in the absolute impossibility of grading the detailed accounts in any degree in accordance with the merits of the subjects in hand. The sketches must vary in length simply as matter of interest has been obtained bearing no relation whatever to the position of the artist in the art.

In this connection it is most seriously regretted that throughout the State many ladies, undeniably superior artists, with knowledge, talent, and possibilities rarely combined, have insisted upon holding themselves aloof from art as a profession, embracing it in the studio, rebuking it in the street. That the right to chronicle their achievements is thus withheld is unfortunate. That the influence, inspiration, and enthusiasm with which proficient and intelligent ladies, in large force, might surround the art-life of the State, are refused, is more than unfortunate. It is a grave question, whether the ability of the artist, having been bestowed, is rightfully wrapped in a napkin, locked up in a private studio for the sole pleasure and benefit of a circle of friends. Those who can do the most for art are eminently those who have not the grinding necessity for bread as the principal pigment upon every palette. Yet those who can, free-handed, labor for glory, are oftener those who shrink into seclusion, letting the art go its way, reliant upon others less able, more willing, for support, so long as they receive the marvellous recreation and enchantment in its rare society. There is also a certain restraint naturally placed on any endeavor to speak plainly of the living. Nevertheless, there being no incentive or desire either to flatter or defame the living or the dead, it must be sufficient explanation to state that those of the present will be regarded precisely as those of the past, and what is said be said with no more consideration that it will ever be read by the subject of the biography than if the last item of the record were taken from an inscription on a marble slab.

A timely suggestion is contained in Whittier's lines : —

> " Of all sad words of tongue or pen,
> The saddest are these, ' It might have been.' "

This thought is often, one might almost say always, present in one shape or another with the artist of sufficient merit to understand his own faults, and is with much truth attributed in some way to the lack of public sympathy. In view of this oftener just than unjust charge, it is but common charity that we base our estimates, especially in the case of artists who are dead, upon their excellences rather than their deficiencies. Such excellences it will be the aim of these papers to detect, avoiding more than a mention of weaker points. The chief desire will be, neither to criticise, nor to fix any estimate of individual or comparative ability, but, in presenting all facts of interest that can be gathered concerning the art-life of each devotee, to trust to the principle, that acquainting the public with the man may assist in the forming of individual criticisms and estimates that shall be of value not only for the past, but in the future. Therefore these papers, taking up the artist only as a part of art, shall make no pretensions whatsoever to any thing more. Nor shall the popular comparisons be instituted between the work of Connecticut artists and that of European masters, either contemporary artists or of ages past, or with the work of other American artists. Such comparisons are entertaining ; when favorable, flattering ; when unfavorable, energizing, perhaps. But, on the whole, they are irrelevant ; and as, with possibly one branch excepted, the highest praise bestowable upon American art is that it approximates the work of certain old masters, jealousy tempts the subject into silence, while other methods are tested to raise the standard of art in our own dear land, till that time shall come, of which the hopeful prophets already detect betokenings, when America may beckon Europe, old masters and new, into realms unexplored by them, and an originality that shall be theirs to copy instead of ours to equal. The facts presented shall be only those concerning the artists as artists of Connecticut, and of which no known doubt exists. The pride and patriotism of the people of Connecticut must be depended upon, who, knowing the artist, or of him, and having seen his work, or at least being able to see it for themselves, shall appreciate a closer view of the homespun web that surrounds him ; and who, knowing him better, and his work better, shall perchance love him more, and prize his work with a more profitable appreciation. If this end be reached, a great success will have been gained.

There are several important galleries of art in the State, of both public and private collection. It was an original intention to include a detailed account of them ; but the fact that most of the important pictures, not of foreign origin, embraced by them, will appear in the course of the biographies, urges the abandonment of the idea. Brief historical sketches of the two best known collections, in the Yale Art Building and the Wadsworth Athenæum, will be alone inserted.

CONTENTS.

MISCELLANEOUS.

FEMALE ARTISTS.

PAINTERS AND SCULPTORS.

Contents.

Contents.

Contents. xiii

CATALOGUE OF ILLUSTRATIONS.

ART AND ARTISTS IN CONNECTICUT.

PREAMBLE.

ONE of the three pioneers in original art in America, Connecticut, entered more vigorously into the field than either of her sister States; though she cannot claim at the outset to have attained the eminent artistic ability of one of her competitors. She produced the first, and for years almost all, of the standard historical works of the country. She has given the world more artists of acknowledged ability than any other State; and from the outset her sons have either led the van, or appeared in the front rank of the nation. The first academic art-school of the country is in Connecticut. In one year, five out of six successful applicants for the title of academician before the National Academy of Design were natives of the State; and to-day over two hundred of the art-students in New-York City, aside from many abroad, are from Connecticut; still the largest number in the field, so far as can be ascertained, from any of the States. Not only has she been thus productive of artists, but also a popular resort where many other great men in art have worked. In this way an important influence has been exerted over even the secluded portions by many of the leading artists of the nation. Coming in contact with the thoughts, theories, and work of masters in the profession, an art-feeling has sprung up, of unusual depth and extent, even in many undisturbed villages. This intimacy has done what the schoolmaster is not allowed to attempt. It has imparted a knowledge which no text-books of to-day contain. It is invaluable as an open-sesame to the richest blessings of civilization, and a promise of even more and better artists for the constantly-increasing facilities. It has planted in the hearts of the people an experimental knowledge and understanding love for that which is truest and best of the work of men's fingers.

The arts of design are with man, and as truly a part of him as his life-blood; frequently developed, but oftener sadly neglected. There is not to be found a nation where painting or picture-making after some fashion does not exist and has not existed. It is, in fact, in the case of every prehistoric nation, the first record of its life, and the earliest chronicle of its being. It is also the invariable exponent of a nation's power. It indicates, through its relics of the past, the rise and decline of its patron ; and, in the present, expands precisely as the nation rises in civilization. The history of art-unions, compared with the history of nations, and their relative positions in the scale of civilization, their chronological superiority, their individual popularity, their national importance, forms an excellent illustration of this fact.[1]

Holding such an important position, it is vitally unwise for either nation or individual to favor any measure that may prove discouraging to art, and eminently advisable to support such measures as shall stimulate it. It is a subject that cannot be handled with carelessness. It depends too entirely upon mutual support to be defrauded of one jot of patronage. Yet the course of America in this respect is something that may with propriety be questioned. The intelligent admirer is no less important to the success of art than the intelligent artist. Either without the other is an impossibility. Both must lie dormant if one will not rise. Progress cannot be made while the arts and the people fail to appreciate each other. The opinion of the sensible lover of art elevates the artist. The work of the good artist educates the critic. In this same connection, a most unfortunate obstacle is placed before the American artist. The true, professional art-critic is the royal interpreter of art for the people, and the bearer of the people's opinion to the artist, — a most important person to both. In Germany, in England, his position is looked upon as next, if not equal, to the artist whose work he faithfully explains and criticises. In America there are many who would boldly assert that there is not a single native-art critic in the land. This may be overdrawn : it is to be hoped it is. But surely they are very few, who, with the knowledge and ability, have not been persuaded, either by fancy or bribery of some sort, to desert American art altogether, unless to compare it disparagingly with imported work. Those who have not made themselves foreign-art critics, as a class spend their energy either in blindly lauding or maliciously slaughtering whatever may fall victim to their pens. The same result is obtained in either case. Those true critics are yet wanting, in any number at least, who,

---

1 The United States is strangely an exception to this comparison. By one of those unaccountable performances of the government, the American Art Union, that, founded in 1839, in 1849 had 18,960 subscribers, an income of $96,300, and distributed over the United States 1,010 works of fine art from American talent, was abolished under the act against lotteries. Thus a very large demand for home art-work was cut off. This is one of several causes for the fact that to-day nearly nine hundred American-born artists are living in foreign lands.

gathering the beauties of a picture, will lay them before the public with an intelligent explanation, and who, with equal sincerity and clearness, will depict the faults. With such we might all in time become critics for ourselves, neither dependent upon the dealer, who, for the profit he obtains, is much more ready to dispose of a foreign than a native production; nor upon the popular critic of to-day, who, for various causes, is more willing to talk of foreign art; nor upon ignorant guess-work, relying on the name of the artist or the depth of the frame for the quality of the picture.

Hitherto the artists of America (there are a few illustrious examples) who have reached a point of excellence that must be acknowledged, that would be by foreign countries if not by their own, have done it by fighting against odds and the interposition of wholly unnecessary hinderances. They reach the goal, and receive their laurels, at a time when they care less for them than at any previous hour of their history. They look upon us as enemies and stumbling-blocks that have with difficulty been overcome. Of what value is our praise to them when they have literally forced it from us? It is but the sword of the conquered passed to the conqueror. They need it no longer. It has dulled its edge to thwart them, and failed. In the nature of things, they must continue to contemplate us as simply a vanquished foe, laving the feet of our victor. There is nothing healthful or satisfactory in this; yet it is only a result of ignorance on the part of the public, inability to judge for themselves, and the necessity of taking others' opinions, biassed and prejudiced, as they may come. Though wealth makes *honorable* men, money cannot purchase that which lifts the man above the brute; which raises one nation higher than another; makes one man happier than his richer neighbor; which gives a charm to life, softening its roughest edges, brightening its darkest hours, — love of the beautiful. That home is more artistic where the prints from weekly papers are tacked without frames to the walls, in a choice and system displaying at least an appreciation and sympathy, than the mansion where a host of pictures are indiscriminately hung and set, graded by, and apologies for, the frames that surround them. Intelligent sympathy elevates the standard of art. Ignorance, no matter how sympathetic, is injurious. The artist who produces that which is worthy of admiration, the critic who honestly translates it, the public bestowing honor where honor is due, — all conspire to the highest civilization; and each endeavor tends equally to raise the art of the country to a higher standard.

This growth of art in a state or a nation is very desirable: for art is not only a great civilizer; it is a great moralizer. Ruskin says, "Art is not only moral, but little else than art is moral." He is at least right so far, that, without industry, a life is a life of guilt; and that, without art, industry is brutality. One reads more of history, chivalry, romance, or villany, in a glance at a picture, than in a day over a novel. A bad book may be read and forgotten, but a bad picture not. Every picture, no matter what it is, tells a story. It tells it more clearly, more concisely, more forcibly, and consequently more lastingly, than it can be told in any other way. This is the most powerful of all arguments for every public and private endeavor to elevate a nation's art; and that history achieves a noble end, well repaying the arduous labor of compiling it, that, being a record of the past, becomes an inspiration for the future to warm a single breast with patriotic enthusiasm, create one new sympathizer for original talent, or recall a single patron of foreign art to a knowledge that infinite possibilities are centred in America.

At present, America seems more ready to accept the work of a foreigner, after paying the cost of importing, than the work of her own children, save of a very few who hold the highest grade. Millions of American money fall into European coffers for originals of the old masters, frauds on the old masters, copies of the old masters, in a mania that reaches even to absurdity, regardless of the continual blows paid thereby to American originality. European art may be better than American. In justice to circumstances, it should be vastly better in comparison than it is. But there is a philosophy as well as policy in the patronage of art, that must sit in judgment with the knowledge even of an expert. There is more in the filling of a gallery than the collection of indiscriminate canvases to cover the space required. There are other matters for consideration than the individual merits of pictures. Justice, common consent, patriotism, demand more. That artist encouraged by the public will grow; while he who is continually neglected, no matter what his genius may be, is belittled and injured. If we would have great men in art, we must make them great. They must win their laurels through us, by us, from us, not in spite of us. The task of the growing, aspiring artist is a hard one at the best. He has great excellences before him to rival if he would become a leader. There is every opportunity for effective, intelligent, sympathetic patronage.

AN OUTLINE OF THE GROWTH OF ART IN CONNECTICUT.

Strictly speaking, the arts of design never began, and will never end. From the fig-leaf aprons to the last sepulchre, they direct the labor of head and hand. The art of painting in America began with the red man's body frescoing, and in the colonies was hardly younger than the earliest settlements. Cotton Mather speaks of an English limner and his sitter for a portrait in Boston in 1667. There have also been the briefest accounts brought down concerning a few native painters, not of sufficient merit to justify a memory, who lived in the early part of 1700. But there was not art-feeling enough in the world at that time to have warmed the soul of one Raphael. The first art-love and labor of importance, as leaving a record of influence behind, that sprang from the virgin soil of America, was not until the middle of the eighteenth century.

In 1728 Dean Berkeley, the most potent of the early patrons of Yale, reached this country from Ireland, bringing in his party John Smybert, a painter. Art was at a low ebb in England, and Smybert was not a prodigy. He had studied from Vandyke, however, and in spirit brought his master's work for the first time to America. To such an extent was this true, that Benjamin West, one of the first to take up the mantle of Smybert, though he studied him probably only through his pictures, bore, in his earlier work, the most evident traces of Vandyke.

Smybert was a better educated than talented artist. His famous work, " The Berkeley Family," now in the Yale Art Gallery, displays more the touch of a man who knew by experience and teaching what certain causes must effect, and whose brush was more the brush of a mechanic, than a man moving in a sphere of originality above his teachers. But it was wonderful work to be seen in America ; probably better than the average of the best English works of the day. It was an inspiration. There may have been many men before in whom the fire of Angelo wanted only a lighting-spark, but did not receive it.

From 1728 to 1751 John Smybert divided his attention between New Haven, Conn., Newport, R. I., and Boston, Mass., settling at last in Boston ; leaving there when he died his son, Nathaniel Smybert. Old Yale — then New Yale — was the scene of his school-days, though he was only a temporary student. Boston claims him as being the grandson of Dr. Williams, the old Latin teacher of the Hub. There his best work was done, and there his bones were laid. He promised a most remarkable future, but died while hardly on the threshold of his career. Blackburn (of Connecticut), Benjamin West and Copley, Col. Trumbull and Ralph Earl (of Connecticut), Gilbert Stuart, Malbone, and Washington Allston, in chronological order, retain the glory of being the first great artists of America. Strictly speaking, then, the history of original art in Connecticut begins with the influence of John Smybert, Blackburn, Col. Trumbull, and Ralph Earl.

The standard of art in the State has been affected by various vicissitudes; but the tendency has been upward.   There has not always been a national leader from Connecticut so boldly in front as Trumbull of the first, and Church of the last generation; but prominent men throughout have represented her, and left a record of increasing numbers and ability.

The position of Blackburn is uncertain, as will be seen hereafter: but after him it is certain that Earl and Trumbull followed, as direct results of Smybert and Copley's influence; and Copley was taught by Blackburn. Malbone, following this influence, in the very last of the eighteenth century visited Connecticut with his famous talent devoted to miniature-portrait painting.   Tisdale was the next in succession.   His art-feeling was due in part to his townsmen Trumbull and Earl, they being prominently figure and historic painters, and Tisdale's first work the same, but chiefly to Malbone, whose miniature portraits he copied, and in which branch he developed his strongest power.   The country was now reviving from the terrible devastation and depression of the Revolutionary war.   A strange fact noticeable to every student of cause and effect and practical results in the world's history, though apparently inconsistent, is an increase of refinement, a revival in æsthetics, a marked progress in the fine arts, after every such conflict and the melancholy season following.   The present enthusiasm in art-interests, following upon the Rebellion, is no exception, but perhaps according to an invariable rule.

This strong head-block for the art of Connecticut, in Trumbull, Earl, and Tisdale, and Stewart (J. R.), in fact, who, though not superior in art, was much for the time, was planted directly after the Revolution.   Gideon Fairman, John Coles, Anson Dickinson, Munger, Waldo, George Freeman, followed in rapid succession in the three departments in which examples had been set them.   Samuel Morse, then in Yale College diligently laying the foundation for his vast achievements in telegraphy, came within this circle; and the native talent that had exhibited itself when he was but four years old was fired to such an extent, that, when the day for his selection of a profession came, he wrote to his father, "I am cut out to be an artist."   His teacher, Allston, introduced him in London to the wonderful art of modelling in clay.   With this knowledge, illustrated in his world-renowned "Dying Hercules," he returned to New Haven. Hezekiah Augur was by nature endowed with the requisite qualities; but it was not until he received the direct *advice* from the lips of Morse that he turned the ability toward marble, and became the first native sculptor of Connecticut.   Thus another branch was introduced.   The chain so firmly fastened now rapidly became strong with many good links.   Fisher, William Jewett, Daniel Dickinson, Jocelyn, Munson, Osgood, Sheffield, and Alexander, born within the eighteenth century, all definitely drew their inspiration from the same sources. Seth Cheney, having learned at home the art of engraving, and being a natural draughtsman, went to Paris, the paradise of crayon-drawing, to pursue his studies of engraving. He could not have avoided drifting into the use of the crayon, and returned to champion, not only in Connecticut, but in America, another branch of art. Thus crayon-drawing was virtually first introduced into the State, and soon obtained many devotees. Thomas Cole next visited Hartford, as, in a sense, a *protégé* of Daniel Wadsworth. Cole was pioneering the way into landscape-painting, and thus virtually introduced another branch as an individual study. H. C. Flagg and F. S. Jewett, both sailors born, were the first distinctive marine-artists of the State. Born in the last half of the eighteenth century were twenty-three native Connecticut artists, nineteen of them after the Revolution. Born in the first quarter of the nineteenth century were forty-eight male and fifteen female artists. Now the field is open wide. There is no longer a possibility of tracing the influence in individual cases, except by individual testimony or distinguishing characteristic; nor any longer a possibility of defining the precise progress and course in the state as severed from the nation.

The time has fortunately passed when passion shall lie dormant for want of inspiration; when ignorance shall crush the artist born, unless, from sheer impossibility to remain under a bushel, the enthusiasm burst its confines in a struggle for the light. The days are dead, happily dead, when the child of art must fight perhaps his hardest battles with himself, not so much as knowing what art is, nor having seen a single valuable picture. Groping in the darkness after light is the most discouraging of all labor. Doubtless many have given up the task, and lived and died comparatively worthless in the world, not even themselves knowing what they were lacking. Hence much of the spice of romance is lost from the artist's life that savored it a century ago. The struggle, the groan, the flush of victory, the shout of triumph, are not so frequent to-day; and to the artist himself his career seems even more prosaic, as a rule, than to his friend. There is an importance, however, in every step of progress made, and every new toiler for glory, that still shrouds each history of a life with intensest interest to the lover of art.

A HISTORY OF THE YALE ART-GALLERY.

The first important art collection in Connecticut was opened to the public in 1831, under the control of Yale College. The gallery was in a small building erected for the purpose at a cost of four thousand dollars. It consisted of a few works of art from time to time gathered by the university, including Smybert's "Dean Berkeley's Family" and the Trumbull Gallery, just secured to the college. The manner in which Yale became possessed of the Trumbull pictures has been presented in various lights, but is of no great importance. Col. Trumbull professed to think that he gave them. Yale College supposed that she bought them. This was only two ways of describing the same transfer. Col. Trumbull being left a widower, and finding old age impairing the cunning of his right hand for new productions, half in anger, half in melancholy generosity, offered his entire remaining collection (doubtless containing some of his most admirable work) to Yale College, on condition that he should be

YALE ART-BUILDING.

paid fifteen hundred dollars a year for the rest of his life, either from the income of exhibition or some other source. This proposition was accepted, and the first public art-gallery begun. Of the artist much will be said hereafter. His gift consisted of several large pictures too intimately known to the people of Connecticut to warrant comment, and two hundred and fifty portraits. Most of the portraits are especially valuable as being of the prominent men of the Revolution with whom Col. Trumbull was personally acquainted, and having been painted from life. They are the first copies, made while collecting portraits for his many famous historical works. Other pictures have been occasionally bought by the college, and others from time to time added by gift and loan. The collection received no marked impulse until the year 1857. Then an incident occurred described later, in connection with the Yale Art School, which brought about in its time a munificent donation by A. R. Street for the present elaborate building, where the gallery was placed in 1866. In 1867 a temporary exhibition of loaned works of art, under the management of a committee of public-spirited citizens of New Haven, was held, and did much to introduce this new feature to public notice, and to interest the people in its growth. The proceeds amounted to over four thousand dollars, — seven hundred dollars in excess of expenses. This was devoted to the purchase of a series of casts illustrative of different stages of plastic art among the Greeks, designed to be the foundation of a collection covering the whole history of sculpture. In the spring of 1868 the well-known "Jarves Collection," illustrative of Italian painting from the tenth to the sixteenth century, was placed in one of the galleries for a term of years. This was a very important accession to the means of instruction in the school, a complete gallery in itself, and an addition that naturally attracted much attention from visitors. A few years since this fine collection was purchased by the institution on favorable terms, and now forms part of the permanent gallery. The Jarves Collection consists of about one hundred and twenty pictures, a few of which are by unknown artists, painted on wood, with gold backgrounds. They are illustrative of the rise of Christian art in Western Europe. The progress of Italian painting is closely followed in this collection. The series commences with contemporaries of Cimabue and Giotto, and contains those of Veronese and Giorgione, illustrating the most interesting period of modern art. Many of the best pictures in the gallery, not belonging to these two specific collections, are from the brushes of Connecticut artists, and will be referred to during the course of the biographies. Beside the paintings there is a large collection of casts and marbles, including some exceedingly interesting and valuable original work. Bartholomew's bas-reliefs of "Adam and Eve," designed for the pedestal of his famous "Eve Repentant," form an important feature.

THE WADSWORTH ATHENÆUM GALLERY.

The Athenæum Art Association in Hartford, like all progress in art a half-century ago, was slow to obtain shape, even after the idea assumed proportions of dignity. Daniel Wadsworth, son of Col. Jeremiah Wadsworth of Revolutionary fame, was, in his early life, the most influential art-lover in the State. Col. Trumbull was an uncle of Mrs. Wadsworth; and his influence may in part account for the fine taste engendered in her husband, as displayed not only in his choice selections, but in his eagerness to extend the benefits of his collection beyond his immediate circle of friends. The subject had long been under discussion in one form or another, when, in 1842, Daniel Wadsworth offered to contribute a lot, facing one hundred and twenty feet on Main Street and one hundred and twenty feet deep (this was extended fifty feet in depth when the demands of the building were estimated), toward the founding of a place that should be devoted to the collection and exhibition of the fine arts. This land was the site of the residence of his father, Col. Wadsworth. In accordance with this the present Athenæum building was erected, the original

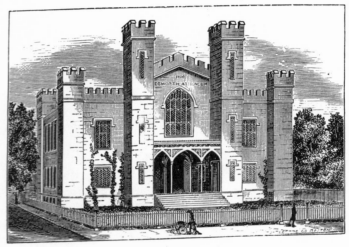

WADSWORTH ATHENÆUM.

being extended, through the influence of Alfred Smith, to compre-
wing for a library, and another for an historical collection. Mr.
th finished the gallery at his own expense, and contributed as a
ber of excellent paintings. Col. Trumbull's works in posses-
Art-Union Gallery had been sold at auction, with the excep-
n pictures. Among these were some of great value as good
he artist's work. A subscription was taken up, in which
, Alfred Smith, and Daniel Wadsworth, were large con-
se pictures were purchased. This, with a few other
s by subscription, formed the gallery, which was
arly in 1844. The paintings were still private prop-

erty, or owned proportionately by subscribers. On the death of Mr. Wadsworth, it became evident that the gallery was in danger of going to pieces. Many of the remaining subscribers presented their portions to form an association, and raised by subscription sufficient to purchase the shares of those less generous. The collection comprises some superior works of art. Connecticut names are prominent in the list. Among the works from out of the State deserving especial attention are Wichelo's "Destruction of Jerusalem," Vanderlyn's "Death of Miss M'Crea," a portrait of Rembrandt Peale by candle-light, a full-length portrait of Benjamin West when president of the Royal Academy by Sir Thomas Lawrence, and many others. This gallery, if not the birthplace, has been at least the cradle, of many ideas in art. Frederick Bartholomew did his first work there while acting as custodian, using the small unoccupied room as a studio that now contains the world-renowned casts and marbles of his later production. These were purchased after his death, and, with occasional additions, — together with a large marble figure of his "Eve Repentant," which was produced after his death, on an order for the Athenæum, from his original model, and by workmen who had helped him upon the first, — form an interesting collection of plastic art. A large subscription toward this purchase was made by Col. Samuel Colt. The Wadsworth Athenæum Association possesses in all two hundred and seventy-five works of art, representing a value of from sixty to eighty thousand dollars.

Unfortunately this gallery is not self-supporting; which fact is used by many as an argument against the expenditure of any thing more upon it. The people will not appreciate what they have, it is said: why do more? There is a certain amount of infant philosophy in this, and much lack of common sense. A gallery, to be attractive, should constantly present something new, — not necessarily every thing new. The public is not, and under the present system cannot be, well enough educated to study one picture untiringly for a much longer time than the artist worked in painting it. There is no inducement to make repeated visits to the same old collection, when one sees but the outlines that apparently make up a picture. The attention of the authorities should also be called to the fact, that, for a valuable gallery, the pictures are very improperly cared for.

A HISTORY OF THE ART-SCHOOLS OF CONNECTICUT.

The Yale Art School, the first and in many respects still the most prominent school of the sort in the United States, is at least an excellent example of the extent to which this valuable system of culture has been adopted in America. Following is a brief sketch of its birth, growth, and present condition. The Yale Gallery had been in existence for some time, when, in 1858, an incident of comparatively little moment proved of great importance, as forerunner and instigator of the Yale School of Art, Members of the Yale Linonian (literary) Society had determined to expend a certain sum on a work of art to adorn their hall. Frederick Bartholomew the sculptor, then in Rome, was asked to make the selection; and through his influence two copies of marble statues from the antique were purchased, — "Demosthenes" and "Sophocles." To welcome the arrival of such royal strangers, a loan exhibition was arranged and held in Alumni Hall for two months in the summer of 1858. Seven thousand visitors examined the collection. Such an enthusiasm was created, that the exhibition resulted in a recognition, on the part of the officers and friends of Yale, that the important influence which art-culture might exert upon college students rendered it desirable as a branch of study in an academic course. Another result was a course of art-lectures, delivered by Professor Salisbury of New Haven, Mr. Deming of Hartford, Professor Greene of New York, Professor A. D. White of Michigan (now President of Cornell University), and Donald G. Mitchell. This movement led to a renewed interest throughout the community, and a more urgent desire on the part of the leading men of the college to establish a separate department of art for broader and more varied culture. This desire had been felt for some time; yet the way was not opened for such a movement until the summer of 1863, when Augustus Russell Street, a wealthy and public-spirited citizen of New Haven, came forward with the generous offer to erect, at his own expense, a building to be devoted to art and artistic studies. Just here Nathaniel Jocelyn, still a venerable and energetic upholder of art in New Haven, should not be forgotten. Mr. Jocelyn's influence has been powerful for art throughout his long residence in the city; and Mr. Street many times confessed that it was chiefly through suggestions and appeals of Mr. Jocelyn that the fact of this important lack was impressed upon his mind. Hence, in a sense, the art-school owes its existence no less to Mr. Jocelyn than to its founder, Mr. Street. This was the first practical expression of the growing conviction that the study of art came within the scope of a great university. His aim was, not simply to found a museum, but to establish a school for practical instruction in art for those of both sexes who were desirous of pursuing the fine arts as a profession, and to awaken and cultivate a taste for and appreciation of the arts among the undergraduates and others.

The corner-stone of the large and costly edifice now known as the Yale Art Building was laid in November, 1864. It was completed in 1866, under supervision of the architect of the National Academy of Design in

New York. It is of revived Gothic, — an adaptation of the thirteenth century to the customs and materials of to-day. The basement contains drawing and modelling rooms. The first story has studios, class-rooms, and library. In the second story is the gallery, well lighted from the roof. The expense of the building was $175,000. The founder died a few months before its completion. The greatest want that now appeared for the perfecting of this design was a thoroughly competent head, capable of conceiving what such an institution should be, and of shaping its incipient developments, as well as of directing art-instruction in theory and in practice. Such a man was found in Professor John F. Weir, an artist of established reputation, who was elected to the directorship of the school in 1869, and immediately returned from his studies and travels in Europe to enter upon the duties which he has since successfully fulfilled. At the same time, Professor Eaton, a graduate of Yale College of the class of 1860, was appointed to fill the chair of the history of art. In 1870 a second general exhibition of pictures was opened. It may prove of interest hereafter, that, at this second exhibition, among the noteworthy guests were R. W. Hubbard, the celebrated landscape-painter of New York (a native of Middletown), and the late John F. Kensett.

In 1870 a large purchase of casts was made in Europe, and from time to time the collection has steadily increased with the addition of well-selected examples of plastic art. In October, 1871, an endowment was secured for a professor of drawing; and John H. Niemeyer, a student of the École des Beaux-Arts, Paris, was appointed to fill the position. Subsequently Mr. Frederick R. Honey was appointed instructor of geometry and perspective. The chair of anatomy is filled by Dr. J. P. C. Foster, resident-physician of New Haven; the chairs of sculpture and architecture being still vacant.

The general objects of the school, as stated in the college catalogue, are the cultivation and promotion of the formative arts, painting, sculpture, and architecture, through practice and criticism. The school is open to all above the age of fifteen, without regard to sex. It already affords a thorough system of instruction in drawing and painting; while courses of lectures on the philosophy, history, and practice of art, are delivered during the college-year. The school possesses a collection, numbering over three hundred, of Braun's "autotypes," which are of great value in promoting its objects.

The art-movement at Yale has advanced until the aggregate of property represented by this department amounts to over $300,000, originating with perhaps the largest single gift from a private source, for the promotion of an institution for instruction in art, in any country. The benefits of this institution are open to the whole country; for the department, while connected with the college on the one hand, on the other receives into its schools all who desire its instructions. A charge of twelve dollars per month for each student is made, and this furnishes the means of providing the necessary models for instruction. The same privileges are extended to students in this department as those accorded students in all other departments of the university. Notwithstanding all of the facilities, however, the lack of home patronage and sympathy still appears. There are a large number of Connecticut students abroad; there are over two hundred Connecticut students in New-York City; while there are but thirty-two regular students in New Haven. Perhaps they are waiting for the Yale school to grow, till it shall become the fashion to attend there. It would be the same stamp of reasoning whereupon we are waiting, and always have waited, for our artists to grow.

There was a struggle toward a school of art in Hartford in 1862. After meeting, and gravely discussing the needs and results of an artists' association, it was decided to compose such a society, and that the study of an egg should be the standard of admission, with various requirements and limitations. Officers were chosen, and the artists very generally entered upon the competitive examination. Some excellent oil eggs are upon canvases scattered over the United States to-day, immortelles of that trial. Some found an egg too high art for them. Some who might have found it too high considered it too low, and did not attempt it. Altogether, like its nursery-famed predecessor, Humpty Dumpty, this art-egg had a great fall; and, as there were no king's oxen and no king's men in a republic, no one ever attempted to set it up again.

The Connecticut School of Design presents an interesting corpse that much needs reviving. The society was formed in 1871 under the name of "The Hartford Art Association." The experiment seemed to promise success; and the association was incorporated in May, 1872, as the Connecticut School of Design, with full powers, and a sufficient capital for beginning work. The members and honorary members included the best artists and many prominent men. There was considerable enthusiasm created at its birth. The exhibition of 1872 in the Charter-Oak Life-Insurance Building was a complete success. One hundred and twenty-eight paintings were loaned, and all tokens seemed to promise fair weather and good speed to the young art-school. Among the artist-members to contribute to this exhibition were W. R. Wheeler, R. M. Shurtleff, Henry Bryant, J. W. Stancliff, N. A. Moore, George F. Wright, S. S. Lyman, D. W. Tryon, Robert Brandigee, G. R. Turnbull, O. Abbiati, Charles N. Flagg, Bryant and Rogers, R. T. Sperry, E. C. Kellogg, T. H. Bartlett, C. H. Meuth,

Miss Ellen M. Pomroy, and Miss E. A. Marsh. But the Connecticut school was started a few years too early to insure success. The tide was not at its flood. The remaining workers in the good cause became weary, and little more than the skeleton of the corporation for instruction in art remains. Still the fact that there is such a society in legal form, possessing a fine selection of casts and a good array of members, and representing a high grade of artistic talent, should inspire the public to an enthusiastic movement in its behalf. There is no danger of overdoing the matter of art-education. What the public-school system will not attempt, through timidity and other equally good causes, the people should do for themselves by the aid of art-associations. The free school, which for three years was held in the Connecticut Mutual Building by this society, should be resumed. The casts alone are too valuable to lie idle.

A society and museum of great promise and importance appeared with the centennial year in New Haven, under the title of "The Connecticut Museum of Industrial Art." The benefits to be derived by the artisan from a fundamental education in art need not be repeated. It is sufficient to assert that the objects of this school are to promote the prosperity and artistic advancement of the *industries* of the State. The plan is the same, on a limited scale, as that upon which the South Kensington Museum is founded, a sketch of which is given elsewhere. The Kensington Museum was the outgrowth of shame on the part of the English people that the artistic grace of their handiwork was so far inferior to the productions of France at the industrial exhibition. The result was most favorable. With almost mushroom growth, gracefulness appeared in England; and, at the next exhibition, the energy inspired had even outdone the rival. Beauty had become more common, and grace in usefulness more abundant, in the manufactures of England, than any other nation. America has nothing in her manufactures to be ashamed of, but nevertheless much to learn. It is one of the fairest omens for ultimate success, that the leading manufacturing interests of the State have already bestowed a hearty welcome upon the institution, and will join in a permanent exhibition under its auspices, to which display the entire first floor of the building occupied as the museum will be devoted. Classes in perspective-drawing, in the decoration of stoneware and pottery designed for household use, and in the manufacture of point and Macramé lace, have already been formed; and instruction in other branches will, before long, be given.

The Hartford branch of the Ladies' Decorative Art Society is also a noteworthy item in the art-history of Connecticut. In June, 1877, fifty ladies met in a private parlor to discuss the propriety of such a league in Hartford. There being no demand for a society for the disposal of the decorative work of the poor, it was at last decided feasible to change the general design till it should be for *instruction* in matters pertaining to decorative arts, and make the experiment. This was done in the fall of 1877, a number of ladies guaranteeing to meet the expenses for three months in case of failure. Instruction in various branches of art was begun, and at once enthusiastically patronized. At the end of three months it was found to have been not only self-supporting, but to number one hundred and fourteen members, and have a considerable surplus in the treasury.

WATER-COLOR PAINTING.

Before the advance of photography, miniature-portrait painting has almost disappeared. The work was the painting of a small portrait, often on ivory, sometimes on paper or other material. The general size was somewhat smaller than the photographed head popular to-day, and effected through the medium of water-colors. A most interesting and instructive description of this work was given the world in 1833 by Thomas S. Cummings, so long and intimately connected with the National Academy of Design in New York, now resident in Mansfield, Conn. This valuable essay on miniature portrait-painting is preserved in William Dunlap's "History of the Arts of Design." To it nothing of worth can be added. Water-color on ivory is comparatively lost ; but water-color painting as a branch of art is steadily increasing in popularity. It has excited much enthusiasm in England, where it has been carried to a high state of perfection ; and the fashion has taken a firm hold upon students in America. Many of the sons of Connecticut have become of repute in the art ; and it may not be out of place to add here, not a discussion of any of the questions raised upon the subject, but a brief explanation of the peculiarities of the comparatively little-known water-color painting.

The branch is entirely distinct, and yet closely akin to oil-painting. The difference in material consists in the vehicle used for the conveyance of the color, and the ground upon which the work is done. The colors are originally the same ; one being mixed with oil, the other prepared and applied with water. Oil must, in the nature of things, change to some extent the original color in mixing and drying. Water evaporates, leaving the pure color as applied ; thus allowing the artist to proceed with his work till completed, without waiting for one color to dry in order to apply the brush again, or taking the picture with him to his studio to finish from memory. It also possesses other desirable qualities pre-eminently its own. It obtains a great advantage from its transparency. The paper and the ground-color naturally affect the finish ; giving a peculiar lumi nous quality, a purity of tint and depth of tone, in response to rapid work. In oil, much time is spent in endeavors to produce the transparency, the subtle gradations, and possible atmospheric effects, that comparatively form themselves in water-color. The beauties that are characteristic of water-colors, and in a sense unattainable in oil, are invariably in the thin, pearly lights, where the absence of heaviness peculiar to water is found. The question as to the propriety of the use of body-colors, which is becoming popular, is unsettled. Water-color has beauties of its own, which oil instinctively endeavors to catch; and the more prominently those charms are perfected, the more consistently beautiful is the painting. No one ever watched an oil and water color side by side, as twilight darkened, without detecting another beauty peculiar to the water. It will hold the light, and express itself in exquisite delicacy, long after the other has faded into darkness. Naturally greater care must be taken to protect the water-color than is necessary in the case of oil; but, once protected, one would hardly suggest that it is not permanent, with the cartoons of Raphael, the great works of Michael Angelo, and the famous frescos of Fra Bartolommeo, fresh and well-defined, whose oil-paintings are hard, faint, and feeble. Miniatures and water-colored ornaments that have survived twice the number of years of the oldest oil-paintings are to-day in better condition. Ancient illuminated manuscripts are another good example of the durability of water-color; and the frescos of Giotto, in the Campo Santo of Pisa, which, exposed as they are to the open air, are still fresh in color and distinct, though the walls on which they are painted are crumbling. Even so near our own day as Turner, to compare his oil and water painting is argument enough in favor of the durability of water-color. These examples also illustrate the words of the ancients, so often ridiculed by modern philosophers upon the subject, that oil-colors were for women and children, and water for men.

It would be unjust to charge upon this any derogation of the sublime art of oil-painting. Work may be done in oil which cannot be approximated in water. It may be that there is yet some missing law, which, when discovered, shall render oil powerless as water as a vehicle of color, preserving the masterly work of the day fresh and beautiful as when first lifted from the easel. There is a lively piquancy and effective brilliancy in water that oil cannot well render, giving it great value for sketching; but there is an elaboration, a boldness of touch and manipulation, a minuteness of detail, which fits oil-color for the conveyance of the greatest, the most complex, the most sublime thoughts of art. A glass over a water-color is fortunately necessary; for it improves it. A glass before an oil-painting destroys the effect of that very delicacy and freedom which is its peculiar perfection. It is evidently the servant of man's most definite individuality, and should be made the most enduring monument of his glory.

EDUCATION IN ART.

A passion for pictures is, not without truth, a distinguishing trait of man from beast; but to know a good picture from a poor one is the result of the highest civilization. Ruskin pointedly remarks, "I have no doubt, that, as we grow gradually wiser, we shall discover at last that the eye is a nobler organ than the ear; and that through the eye we must, in reality, obtain and put into form all the useful information we are to have in this world."

Education is required no less by the public than by the artist. It is required by both. The facilities for obtaining it in either case are sadly deficient in America. Unrivalled genius, unequalled taste and suscepti- bility, and the most perfect eye, would be almost idly wasted, unless care- fully educated. They must be possessed of a culture that unfortunately cannot, as a rule, be obtained in this country. The young man of promise goes at once abroad, because he cannot — which is, in great part, due to the primary fact that he will not — submit himself to the rigid discipline at home that there he accepts, and by it becomes a masterly workman. Of necessity, he returns to us, if at all, a foreign artist. A life-long posi- tion at his easel will not suffice to re-instate American originality which has been so laboriously driven out of him. The famous "Swapping Horses," so thoroughly characteristic of America, so purely original, has, doubtless, its faults. They are faults which only a course of strictest study could overcome. That study had to be undertaken abroad. In the course of it American originality was so thoroughly lost, that another picture of the nature of the first was impossible to the artist after his return. He painted better, but he painted as a European. Schools we *must* have; and a complete system of schools is what we can have only when the public are satisfied to sacrifice their passion for European work, and give encouragement to educate from among themselves men who are perfectly capable of being masters in art. Schools with voluntary courses are becoming common in America to-day. The pupil practises as it may please him upon one model or another, in one style or another, at one hour or another, under one teacher or another, for a month or a year. The schools we need are such as our students of France and England know, where the grinding and the grovelling wipe out the romance and the poetry of color altogether, till the first steps in art are thoroughly mastered. It is by no means intended to assert here that we have no art-schools ; for undoubtedly we have some that are very superior. Connecticut may well pride herself upon one of the best in the United States : but their dignity is low, through lack of appreciation ; they are crippled by prejudice ; they are injured by lack of patronage. All that can justly be said against the schools of America is, that they are undeveloped.

Connected with the British Royal Academy is an art training-school, with Edward Armitage as professor of painting ; Weekes, of sculpture ; Barry and Spiers, of architecture ; Calder Marshall, of anatomy ; Barff, of chemistry ; and Bowler, of perspective. The South Kensington Museum, established in 1852 "for the purpose of training art masters and mistresses for the United Kingdom," to use the words of the founders, is doubtless the most remarkable school of the sort in Christendom. Annual appropriations from Parliament are bestowed upon it : and, for ten months in the year, day and evening schools are in full operation, with two complete outfits of models and apparatus ; it being considered both wise and well that male and female students should study art separately. There are elementary drawing-classes, night-schools for artisans, and instruction in all of the higher branches, beside the training-school for teachers. They have competitive examinations of a most searching character, that the knowledge gained may be tested upon its practical side in its scientific principles. Allowances are made for the maintenance of the pupils of from one hundred and fifty to four hundred dollars annually, and the graduate is considered qualified to teach in any similar school in the kingdom. Members of the extra classes alone number one thousand three hundred. An extensive art-library and a superb ceramic art and scientific collection is connected with the museum, as well as a distinct collection of oil and water-color paintings. In short, there are in England six hundred and seventy-five art-schools, instructing fifty thousand pupils. Corresponding examples might be cited from Germany and France, but are too well known to admit of repetition.

The subject of art-education, from the very fact that some attention is already paid to it in the State, becomes one of special importance. There has been no time in our history when such a deep interest has been taken in art as to-day. He may not claim the gift of prophecy who predicts that we are entering upon a period of art-development that shall crystallize the chaotic jumble, and reduce to a system the unorganized resources and talent of the land. When we are once thoroughly engaged upon the subject, we shall create art-schools, that, in the nature of things, will become superior to those which are the pride of the Old World to-day. The time will not come suddenly, nor yet for the asking ; nor, on the other hand, will it come if we sit comfortably watching the weathercock and barometer.   Manifest destinies are always accomplished by the meeting half way of that inexorable "must be," which mysteriously will be, and yet can be only by the will of free agents.   Art has its system of growth and its laws of life; but, whatever the omens may foreshadow and the oracles assert, it is useless to look for an important progress till the fountain of enthusiasm shall take its source in the hearts of the people.   The historic and ethnic principles which have caused the present European schools need not be repeated.   Spontaneity is the soul of art, individuality its life, intelligent sympathy its inspiration and support.

Progress rests with individual, non-professional labor, quite as much as with the artist; yet one would be ridiculed who should suggest that art in all its branches be introduced and made a compulsory study in our primary, grammar, high schools, and colleges.   But while it may be an exaggerated view that any one, with proper instruction, can become a good vocalist, or an entertaining performer upon any musical instrument, it may be, nay, must be, conceded that none but a blind man can study drawing honestly and well without being made thereby, in a sense, an artist.   Every good picture a man sees elevates his taste in just so much as he gives attention to it, and every hour's instruction he has had upon any detail of the art makes every picture so much more an open book to him.   It enhances his interest, instruction, and pleasure, producing another and ever-increasing source of joy that nothing can eradicate.   This is only one result, and a minor one, of introducing the arts of design in the simplest form into a common-school education.

Some of the schools of Connecticut have already branched from the prosaic "Reading, 'Riting, and 'Rithmetic," with the timid advance of an exploring-party; but the prophecy is ventured, that the time approaches when these pioneers will be enthusiastically followed after a fashion that shall make the ghosts of the ferule-armed masters of the old red school-houses stare in consternation.   Every child that lives to study the three immortal " R's " will also have a sound introductory knowledge of that which is in them all and over them all.

Long before the history of art in the State begins, when those who had trodden Plymouth Rock gathered on the shores of the Connecticut, the school was uppermost in their minds.   Almost the first laws enacted regulated the system of instruction, and the ability of the master who must be employed, under penalty of a heavy fine.   Necessarily the fine arts took no position in their calculations.   Naturally they were by them considered a frivolous pastime; a knowledge to be shunned rather than courted.   They must build cabin-walls with logs as best the logs would build them.   They must paste their walls over with mud quickly and durably. They had no time to cover them with canvases. But these primitive notions are items of history, and better so. We have another life to deal with, a higher story to build upon the excellent foundation they laid for us. It has been too long the fault of common-school systems, that too much time was bestowed upon the past, too little upon the present and the future. Men's capabilities lie buried in them, and are oftener discovered when sought for than forced upon the notice of the heedless, ignorant possessor.

It is not alone for the making of the artists, or the creating of intelligent admirers of painting and sculpture, that a knowledge of art is desirable: it is the making of men. It is not an over-statement, that whatever position in life a man be able to fill, from the humblest artisan to the most opulent aristocrat, he can more enjoyably and more profitably fill it for possessing a knowledge of the arts of design. Logically, the comprehension of any creation, be it simple or intricate, a fork and knife or an electric system, tends to its best adaptation to individual or public needs. Artists themselves are a good example. They are not non-utilitarian. Proverbially, the greatest inventors of the world have been artists. This, it is said in explanation, is because their faculties of invention are always in activity before the canvas, and, naturally developed by much exercise, occasionally leap from the confines of the easel. But it is shallow reasoning. The explanation is deeper than that, and at the root of this demand for instruction in art. They are of the chosen few, who, having possessed themselves of a degree of knowledge, have intelligently studied form and fashion, the nature of things, and the adaptability of inanimate figure and combination to the production of grand results, real and ideal, and the creation of that which shall express the greatest thoughts, and most naturally meet the necessities of mankind.

For centuries, universities have labored to add to the mass of information attainable within their walls. They have gathered any thing and every thing that might promise to satisfy the greedy hunger of the seeker after knowledge. Nevertheless, it has become suggestively clearer with every age, that we owe to those outside the influences of universities, who have by force, not encouragement, made of their minds creative instead of dumbly receptive organs, most of the advantages, privileges, and pleasures of our existence over that of the South-sea Islander. One style of cultivation is eminently desirable: the other is positively indispensable. Both must be combined to complete the circle, and this combination is inevitable.

What to-day is stigmatized as "learning a trade," for instance, will some day, in a much more extended and exalted form, be one result of a common-school and college education. People will discover that the lowest and the highest occupations of man are one and the same, after all, — expressions of the arts of design, in which there is a place and a labor for every man that breathes. This place he needs but education to be able to fill. Acquainted with art, he becomes a master instead of a slave ; an artist, a *workman,* than which there is nothing nobler or more divine ; a creative being, possessing in himself infinite resources of satisfaction, and possibilities of eternal progression. Men will discover that they are capable of producing, — a fact which few realize to-day. By broadening the basis of education till it shall comprehend the elements of art, we shall do away with the accidental stumbling through which all great creators have attained their greatness. We shall have placed within the reach of all the first stepping-stones to useful and ornamental careers ; prevented the ignorant wasting of human power, the misdirecting of human life, the temptations of helplessness, unproductiveness, and idleness, to immorality and vice.

It must be remembered here, that no education is intended to make a master. It is not the end of study. It gives the methods, and indicates the means. It produces possibilities, and offers them universally. To return directly to the arts of design, examples are endless of the great benefit derived from popular instruction. For ages, in the common schools of Greece, the youths were trained in both theory and practice in the plastic art ; and the result was Phidias and Apelles. Men of all ranks and classes were long trained in art in modern Italy, preparing the way for Raphael, Michael Angelo, and Leonardo da Vinci. A nation of individuals possessing an independent opinion of works of art also naturally puts a veto upon abortive productions. So long as people will buy poor pictures, there will be lazy artists glad enough to supply them. When there is no market for such, — and there will be none so soon as people are well enough educated in art to know the poor picture from the good one, — as a matter of course there will be no more poor pictures. Thus, in a double sense, art-education in the common school and university would throw the burden of magnifying the nation's ability upon men of talent, and force them to kneel humbly and patiently to Art, till she knelt to them, and acknowledged them master. It would stimulate the bone and sinew of the country. It would produce from the same material better workmen than the foreign schools, and at once preserve to the United States not only the great native genius, but a well-defined originality.

William Hazlitt, the English table-talker, said, "I would rather leave a good portrait behind me than a good biography ; for many circumstances might conspire to prejudice one who should read the biography, but nothing could tinge the portrait but the character of the man it portrayed." None the less is it wise for each generation, as it comes and goes, to leave its most important record, not in history, romance, and poetry, that may be twisted, mangled, and garbled by fashion and prejudice, but in art, that cannot change; and to this end responsibility rests upon every loyal citizen.

It should not, however, be understood that lack of education on the part of the public, and want of sympathetic encouragement for the artist, are the only causes for an apparent lack of original art in America. The fine arts do not pioneer. Painting and sculpture cannot keep pace with advancing civilization, but of necessity must be the very last and highest refinement to be exposed. They are the fruit, not of excitement and necessity, but of repose. It is a fact which none would attempt to deny, that there is but little originality as yet to distinguish the art-life of America. In sculpture we are deficient. In painting we still "look up." In architecture we have produced but a bastard jumble. But in defence be it urged, we are young. We are composed, in the greater part, of emigrants from other nations, — the least artistic of every community. Our fields are not yet half of them planted : shall we carve marble well before we have completed the plough-share? We have not roofs enough to cover the thousands flocking hither-ward from everywhere : shall we devote our energy to monuments and arches, graceful presentations and grand effects, before we have prepared a place to lay our heads? The promise in America is great, the possibilities unlimited. Scarce a hundred years have passed since the fine arts found a first footing in native soil : yet Connecticut has already produced more than one man of whom it may well be said that

" All the world was proud that he was born ; "

and hardly a year passes but higher steps are taken, offering every encouragement to the fullest, freest confidence in hope of further progress.

THE TRUE ARTIST AND HIS WORK.

In conclusion of this general review, it may be allowed to add a few suggestions of common observation upon merits and faults in artists and their work. The great labor of art, as already argued, is to civilize and moralize. That artist most fully realizes art who tunes by it his own spiritual nature. That artist most fully expresses art who makes it an important factor in the common good. A work of art is grand and true as it produces emotions which are ennobling and elevating. By this standard all results of the artist's labor may safely be measured. "Jan Steen," it is said, "found the talk of the ale-house favorable to his painting of pot-house brawls;" but it is the glory of ennobling art, that it cannot be gathered out of corruption. Minor works, executed only as a pastime or relaxation, of narrower range and import than the great works that stamp a country's genius, cannot, of course, be graded as low or high art precisely as they fill, or fail to fill, this requirement; but the tendency of the great artist is to great work, no matter how limited his subject. While the lowest art is "the subordination of nothing to nothing," it is emptiness and nonentity elaborated without object or design; and all forms and degrees of low art savor of this principle. Our country is literally flooded to-day with mercantile specimens both of European and American painting, not art; not imbecile abortions, that fall dead at birth, but specimens, unfortunately, more popular than the true-born child of art, — damaging, demoralizing specimens.

The artist who endeavors to represent ideas, whether successfully or otherwise, is, in proportion to his success, a benefactor to his nation. The spirit and design of the picture are of vastly more importance than the finish. Finish, in fact, is what no work of high art ever attained. It is the picture painted to sell, the picture that unfortunately does sell, that is finished. That work which is an inspiration to the mind of every intelligent observer is not, cannot in justice to nature be, complete in itself, or itself complete. He who bows to the people paints for them a pretty picture, with bright colors, senseless figures, unity without life, law without love, and fine polish arranged in every detail. He to whom the people must bow, if not to-day with their purses in their hands, then to-morrow with a laurel crown, is the artist who has shunned the allurements of this fancy, and endeavored to reproduce emotion and idea from the pure motive of love that has been kindled in his own breast; whose lights have something to illumine, whose shadows something to relieve. Thought is every thing, even to a portrait-painter. There is much truth in that jesting praise, "It looks as though it could speak." There is a compliment imbued with a profounder truth in the words, "It seems to think." The height of portraiture, of art, in fact, is doubtless to produce that which thinks, or sets others thinking. Whether in painting or sculpture, that man who has not a thought in himself, he who is not original, never can be an enduring artist. He who does not add to that originality culture, power of expression, will profit little by it. As every thing that is elevating is noble and pure, he cannot make the great artist, whom the people must acknowledge as prince in the brotherhood, who attempts the highest walks until impelled thereto by lofty thought and the purest conceptions of the true and the beautiful. "A good tree cannot bring forth evil fruit, neither can a corrupt tree bring forth good fruit." Every thing little, mean, or low, must be exorcised from the mind of him who would be a great artist. That which satisfies merely the fancy bows to a fickle sovereign. In short, that art is the highest, that style is the grandest, that does not satify *any thing;* which is only suggestion, it may be either simple or profound; which, in the language of another, "produces the greatest number of ideas." Art is a jealous mistress, and will not long abide by one who neglects her: hence, possessing all other good qualities, he who is not diligent, he who is not subservient, he with whom every circumstance of life does not bend to art, is not worthy of success.

We should know the artist, as well as his work, to whom we would offer allegiance. By knowing him, we shall avoid two great blunders, — that of running with the crowd after any one who may have excited it, and that of falling on our knees before a man scarcely less ignorant of art than ourselves. In the nature of things, art must rely upon justice for ultimate success; but the public is not always just. In matters of art the public is grievously ignorant. People do not take time to consider, but, reliant upon a few leaders, laugh and cry at bidding, quite as the second audience to witness "She Stoops to Conquer" — though the first had hissed it from the stage — was forced to applaud in response to the applause of a prominent friend of Goldsmith, who volunteered to sit in the first box, and literally explain the play by vigorously clapping and laughing in appropriate places. Turner could never have been known and honored as he was had not John Ruskin appeared to explain him, so that people who would not take the time, and did not possess the ability, to judge, might know his work if they would hear his interpreter. It is all the more a good illustration, if it be true that Ruskin, in his uncontrollable enthusiasm and exuberance of language, overdid the matter, and made England think there was a divinity in Turner which he never possessed.

Evidently that is not the best which may at first appear so. If we cannot judge for ourselves of the merits of a picture, we may at least refrain from heedless enthusiasm. And surely a history of artists must have this good effect, that, knowing the man, we may at least be able to curb our judgments of his work. "Out of the abundance of the heart the mouth speaketh." Apparently this is even truer of the artist and his brush. The tongue can deceive: the brush, as a matter of enduring fact, cannot deceive if truly studied. Sir Joshua Reynolds clothed this thought most perfectly when he said, "The chief end toward which every good artist strives is to be able to place himself so perfectly upon his canvas, that he who looks at it shall *see* his thoughts precisely as he thought them." A living artist has said very truly, "The highest art is where there has been most perfectly breathed the sentiment of humanity."

"We receive but what we give,
And in our life alone does Nature live."

Consistency is another vital necessity to the best works of art, and consequently to the artist. In the lavish variety of the most impulsive genius there must yet be a fidelity and unity, or, being inconsistent, though honest perhaps, it can never be trustworthy.

It is no design of this argument to convey a suggestion that art is religious, or artists gods; though that theory is, in a degree, held' by able men. It is emphatically denounced as an error. Art is always moral: religion may be very immoral. Religion deals with the true or the untrue: art deals with the beautiful. Religion is in fact truth, or truth distorted: art is beauty. Truth is for the reason: beauty is for the emotion. Truth is the strength: beauty is the grace. Truth builds: beauty finishes. Æsthetic feelings are often mistaken for religious feelings, but at cost of a great error. The true and the beautiful belong together for the perfection of life; but they are not one, nor can they be.

It is a proverb in art, that every beauty is never expressed in any one model. It is equally probable that all the requirements for the perfect artist will never be gathered in one man. Sometimes a poor draughtsman or a poor colorist, or a man lacking in a part of the spiritual requirements, may take a high position. The nearer the ideal, of course the higher the rank. Copying, in the sense of reproducing another's picture, is here purposely ignored. It is simply parroting in art, which any one with a knowledge of colors can indulge in. Imitation is not art.

Knowledge, as previously urged, is the thing most lacking in America. Without it, culture is as helpless as a sword in the hand of a paralytic. The advancement lately made, however, in the science of the relation of things, gives ample promise of a brilliant future in the United States for painting and sculpture. In landscape especially we may find excellent work in America, even when compared with the best that Europe can produce. This is a natural result of circumstances. There is more of landscape than of any thing else in a new country. Nature is perfect, and, in truth, the only thing that approaches perfection. Since the time of Constable and Turner, landscape-painting has been almost deserted in England. It has degenerated into a feeble mannerism. The German school of landscape-painting is hardly worthy the name. It is not only outrageously mannered, but of wholly mechanical mannerism. Landscape at the best is chiefly the outgrowth of the modern æsthetic mind. It cannot be expected of it that it will always hold the position it has attained in America. Other perfections will come before the aspiring student as forcibly as Nature now presents the landscape. It should not argue against the skill and rank of an artist in America, though it often is thoughtlessly allowed to, that he is not a landscape-painter, simply because that is the prevailing fashion of the day. Of the manner of painting, no less than the subject, is this true. Whatever pigment an artist use, whatever his model may be, it argues nothing but the bent of his personal taste. We must look at his work in the abstract as though it were the only work in Christendom, put ourselves in the artist's place, think with him, see with him, in order to correctly judge his work.

The art-education of the painter is also of great importance. There are what are variously termed born artists, native prodigies, self-taught painters. Occasional supposed representatives of this class, by a brilliant career, have added glory to the titles. But it is hardly for the artist himself to say that he is self-taught, much less his biographer; for education, more especially art-education, may be a subtly-administered blessing. A good picture under favorable circumstances, a word, an example, may have carried years of study in a single impression. Such incidents will often account for the mysteries of unschooled success. The rule remains, that but a limited degree of excellence is attainable without careful instruction. Nature produces the apt scholar: she can do no more. Laws and principles are neither mysteriously planted in native soil, nor will they spring up there at hap-hazard. The faithful student is he who wins the long race in art. With this same thought occurs the value of a life-long labor. George Eliot touched very lightly a profound truth in the course of her story of "Daniel Deronda," where she presents the advice given by Herr Klesmer to Gwendolen after financial disaster had driven her to resolve upon entering the stage. The greatest characters in every profession, the world over, are those who have knelt as devotees from childhood. There are exceptions to this rule, and it is by no means to the dishonor of an artist that he took up his brush late in life. But in itself it is a recommendation for one in any profession, most of all in art, that the position is the outgrowth of a life of industry.

A good artist must be physically a brave man. It is easy to follow a beaten path, to copy another, if not in exact outline, in thought, in manner, and in character; but he only becomes a true artist who dares break from the restraining conventionalities imbibed with education. He is a bold man who stands upon, rather than in, the subtle influence of patronage. He must be independent and courageous who would not sacrifice originality to the public's whim and the critic's fancy. That an artist is poor, is no sign that he is not talented; that he is not popular, is not, unfortunately, an infallible indication that he is not superior to many who are receiving praise of the people. It is not safe to form judgments in matters of art on the opinions of others, nor is it safe to arrive at a conclusion through ignorant fancy.   Mlle. de Fauveau, a celebrated young artist of the political-persecution days of France, curtly wrote to a friend, "We artists are like the Hebrews of old : manna is sent us daily, but on the condition that we save none for to-morrow."

Desirable qualities are not invariably backed by an enthusiasm that will thrust them forward against all opposition and neglect.   There is murder in a word at times.   The possessor of any artistic talent should be protected by the people, not buffeted by them.   The bootblack, the office-boy, the clerk, the dreaming schoolgirl, may shelter unnoticed a flame of art that is destined to be a brilliant light in the future, unless hidden under the bushel of neglect.   Any genuine talent is worthy the freest sympathy of every *intelligent* citizen.

With this the biographical sketches are presented.   Not that the subject of art in the abstract has been comprehended, scarcely apprehended. It were a fatal struggle to endeavor to comprehend that which is limitless. Nor has an exhaustive treatise been attempted : that might well be pronounced a failure.   What has been given is all that was desirable, — simply the basis upon which opinions and suggestions that may follow will be founded.

ARTISTS OF CONNECTICUT.

NATURALLY, the oldest, or more properly the youngest artists, — those identified with the earliest days, — are in proportion the most unsatisfactory subjects of research, with records very difficult to obtain, there being but a single authentic history of the early days of art in America. Naturally, too, if there be any disputed details, they will occur among the first. The channels to celebrity were less available a hundred and fifty years ago, and the means of becoming permanently known out of the reach of any but undisputed prodigies. The occupation of the artist especially was far inferior in the public mind to that of many other men. He was but little better than a beggar and an itinerant, stopping at door and door for work; a boarder, and often an unwelcome boarder, where he painted, in the majority of cases. Though we know that there were talented artists in America a hundred and fifty years ago, we know them more by what we see than by what we hear. Very indefinite knowledge, derived almost entirely from his works, is all that now remains of one of the first painters of rank of America, —

J. B. BLACKBURN.

So soon as the works of Mr. Blackburn, having lain almost forgotten for a century and more, began to revive in popularity, a disagreement arose among his admirers regarding the origin of the man; which, from the length of time since he was forgotten, will probably always remain a disagreement. This is the more unfortunate, because much of his work is to-day highly valued for its intrinsic worth, even when compared with the accomplishments of art that have followed it. At least thirty portraits of Mr. Blackburn's painting are owned in Boston, where he painted either with or directly after Smybert, and for some time following (i.e., from about 1745). Some of his paintings are still owned in Connecticut, and others that must have been painted in the State have migrated with the course of empire. Among them is a large painting of Gov. Saltonstall's

29

family (four of his children), arranged about a table. It is agreeable in design, and finely painted; good in its tone and drawing; and indeed quite remarkable throughout, considering the circumstances. The flesh-tints are neither crude, thin, nor pale, but show a strong sense of the beauty of flesh; while his draperies are striking for ease and grace of line and mass, his background admirable for strength and clearness. These criticisms will apply equally to the most of his work now known to the public. William H. Whitmore, in his Notes on Peter Pelham, says of Blackburn, "In his day, as an artist, he was second only to Copley." There is no doubt that he taught John Copley; and members of the Massachusetts Historical Society advance the theory, that the pupil, improving, rapidly outdid his master, and literally drove him away. At all events, nothing is known of Blackburn, either in Boston, Connecticut, or elsewhere, after 1760. He seems to have "dropped out," leaving no date either of death or departure. Mr. Dunlap, the historian of American art, gives up the task of penetrating, and leaves the artist with the two-line remark, that he painted at one time in Boston, and painted good portraits. Tuckerman at greater length expresses the same lack of information, only diverging to speak of him as a visiting foreigner. But Mr. Tuckerman did not search far enough to discover even the artist's initials, and probably judged of the foreign origin simply by the Scotch vibration to his name, or that good painters of the day were generally foreigners. Sufficient investigation to have assured him that his subject was not of American origin must also have shown him his initials. He printed his name on almost all of his pictures, "J. B. BLACKBURN."

Private authority, in the shape of heir-loom legendary, gives the artist Blackburn a Connecticut origin. We surely possess too many of his works to admit the theory that he only visited America, beside incontrovertible proof that he painted for over fifteen years in Massachusetts, aside from the time he must have spent in Connecticut. In searching for proof to support the Connecticut theory, it has been found that about the year 1703 (before and after) an itinerant painter and jack-at-all-trades, Christopher B. Blackburn, worked in various parts of the State. Certain papers, dated in Wethersfield, would indicate that he was the meagre head of a moderate family living there. These facts prove nothing; but it may be that Christopher B. had a son, J. B., possibly born in Wethersfield, probably about the year 1700. Such a son, — born with perhaps no more talent than hundreds of others, but with a possibility of making the most of it, — receiving the rudimentary knowledge of color from his father, would naturally have gone to Europe to complete the study begun in the wilds of New England under an itinerant limner of no pretensions. Unknown, of course he would have gone away, and returned — what he was called — virtually a foreign artist.

Evidently this is not a propitious biographical beginning, though the result of a laborious research; but the fact that Connecticut offered the United States the first native painter of prominence is a sufficient glory to dignify the slightest items that may form a proof. Hence the above is inserted, and yet not as evidence, but in the hope that it may be a stepping-stone to the uncovering of facts that shall amount to sufficient evidence and undeniable proof.

REV. JOSEPH STEWART.

The next man to register his name in the pages of history as an artist of Connecticut was the Congregationalist minister, Rev. Joseph Stewart. He was born in 1750. He painted a little in New Haven when but twenty years old, while studying for the ministry. Entering his profession, he laid aside his art of painting, till in 1800, driven by ill health from the pulpit, he appeared in Hartford with a collection of curiosities, and opened a museum in an old building still standing on the corner of Main and Talcott Streets. Among this collection were several specimens of Mr. Stewart's painting; and in the museum he set up his easel, becoming also a deacon of the Centre Church. In these various offices he won the respect and confidence of the good people of Hartford, and supported himself, his wife (a daughter of the famous Squire William Mosely), and two reputedly beautiful daughters. He painted for a very low price, but probably received all the work was worth. Dr. Mason Strong's portrait is the best remaining likeness to be found, and is far excelled by the artist's copies of Gov. Saltonstall and the second Gov. Wolcott, now in the Hartford Historical Rooms. The Museum Hall was the wonder of the city, especially of the small boys, who on Saturday afternoon were admitted for five cents each, and allowed to rally round one of the first hand-organs ever brought into Hartford. In time the hand-organ gave in to the boys, and lost some of its best notes; but they enjoyed it none the less. A little later, the museum was united with a larger one; and it and its owner, submerged in an increasing flood, were forgotten.

RALPH EARL.

The name of Earl sorely perplexed Mr. Dunlap, who, in the course of his invaluable history, has several confused statements concerning Earls of whom he had heard in different parts of the country. These several, however, with a few corrections, resolve themselves into a comparatively minute history of a son of Connecticut who very early honored her art.

Ralph Earl (not T. Earl, as appears in Mr. Tuckerman's book) was born in Lebanon, Conn., about the year 1751. Through some misinformation, Mr. Dunlap has him born in Leicester, Eng., where he had relatives, and where he afterward found a wife. What instruction he obtained beyond the study of pictures is uncertain; but in 1771 he was painting miniature and life-size portraits as an itinerant through the State. A townsman, and only older by five years than Col. Trumbull, it is not impossible that many of the same influences bore upon each. This life he pursued till the breaking-out of the war, when he entered the Governor's Guard, and joined in the famous march in defence of Lexington and to Cambridge. When twenty-five years old, an influential friend offered him a chance to study art abroad if he would go in the capacity of a gentleman's servant. The love of art conquered the pride of the soldier, and he went. He remained twelve years abroad, much of the time in London, studying under Benjamin West, and through his influence obtained a commission to paint the portrait of King George III. He was also made a member of the Royal Academy of Art. In 1786 Ralph Earl returned to Connecticut with his wife. A strange similarity in names, dates, and circumstances, led Mr. Dunlap to conjecture that an artist by the name of Earl, who died in Charleston, S.C., of yellow-fever, in 1792, leaving a widow and children in London, was the Connecticut artist. Mr. Tuckerman copied this conjecture, putting it in the positive form of a fact. Whereas Ralph Earl, the Connecticut artist, author of the works that both the above writers credit to their various subjects of the name, died in Bolton, Conn., in 1801. He was a man of recklessly intemperate habits, and literally "murdered his own greatness" with liquor. As a necessary incident, he was a man of very fluctuating fortune; and, though at times "rolling in riches," Mr. Tuckerman relates that once, the artist having been imprisoned for debt, the wife of Gen. Hamilton and others went to the prison, and sat for their pictures to assist in his release. Of the work of Mr. Earl a more accurate estimate cannot be given than that contained in Mr. Dunlap's history, and wisely copied by Mr. Tuckerman, though without giving credit. The wisdom is repeated: "He had considerable merit; a breadth of light and shadow, facility of handling, and truth in likeness." His principal work, and that which alone should make his name famous, is a series of four large paintings from sketches made upon that march of the Governor's Guard. They were the first historical paintings executed by a native-American artist, and were afterward engraved by Amos Doolittle. He also painted Niagara Falls, and a portrait of Col. George Willis that now hangs in the Hartford Historical Rooms. In Hartford he painted a portrait of Judge Ellsworth, and one of Col. Talcott. This latter, of course completed in the colonel's house, was commented upon by his housekeeper at the request of the artist. The criticism was, " It might do well enough for a picture if he didn't sit so bastely in his cheer." Ralph Earl also painted the finest existing portrait of Roger Sherman, now in a private collection in New Haven.

On the artist's return from Europe, Mr. Whiting of New Hampshire engaged him to paint his family ; but he procrastinated so unbearably, and was so entirely under the influence of liquor, that the engagement, as many similar following, was broken off. Finding his sceptre fast departing, though he was hardly in the prime of life, he gathered together what little he had left of money and effects, and retired to a quiet dying-place in the silent old village of Bolton. Of his son Augustus nothing can be found that should entitle him to a place in Connecticut. His wild, roving life forms an excitingly interesting history, full of triumphs and failures ; but he was probably born in London, and left there when his mother followed her husband to America.

JOHN TRUMBULL.

When a man of mark has been dead for the third of a century, and left to the world a full and interesting autobiography, beside several biographies and semi-biographies, it must of necessity be a difficult task to write any thing new of him ; but, in the case of John Trumbull, the time has not yet passed when a general but brief survey of his personal characteristics as an artist and a man may not be both interesting and profitable.

He was the son of Jonathan Trumbull, the Colonial Governor of Connecticut, who was endearingly called " Brother Jonathan " by Washington. He was born in Lebanon, Conn., June 6, 1756 ; and graduated at Harvard College in 1773, when he at once turned his attention to painting. He joined the army in 1775 as an adjutant, and, having rendered some special service by drawing plans of the English fortifications, was made an aide-de-camp to Washington ; served with Gates in the Northern army as adjutant-general, and resigned his commission in 1777. Having resumed the pencil, he went to Paris in 1780 ; thence to London, where he studied art with Benjamin West. While there, he was suspected as being a spy, and was imprisoned for eight months. On being released through the influence of West, he returned to America in 1782. He again visited England, and returned in 1789. In 1794 he went to England as secretary to John Jay, and passed about ten years in the diplomatic service. In 1811 he again visited England, where he remained four years; when he returned to New York, where, with the exception of a brief sojourn in New Haven, he remained until his death, Nov. 10, 1843. In addition to the positions already mentioned, he held that of President of the American Academy of Fine Arts, and, as such, did much to foster the love of art in the United States. As he advanced in years, he collected his unsold paintings into a gallery, which he disposed of to Yale College on the condition that he should receive an annuity of fifteen hundred dollars during the balance of his life; which arrangement enabled him, with other income, to reach the end in comfort and peace.

During this long period, Col. Trumbull was constantly studying, if not practising, his favorite art. Aside from the many portraits and small miscellaneous pictures that he painted for his friends, — of which sixty-eight were painted before he was twenty-five years of age, — there are many always accessible to the public in Washington, Hartford, New Haven, New York, and Boston or Cambridge, ranging in size from miniature to mammoth productions. Of the portraits the largest proportion are not only excellent as works of art, but invaluable as contributions to history. The larger paintings in the national capital, in spite of some deficiencies, must always be highly esteemed because of their subjects; while the eight smaller productions connected with the Revolution, and forming a part of the New-Haven Collection, cannot but command the admiration of the most competent critics. In technical skill Col. Trumbull was of course greatly behind such men as Meissonier and others of that stamp; but, so far as the higher objects of art are concerned, the American undoubtedly stands on a higher plane than the famous Frenchman. That Col. Trumbull was a great master cannot be reasonably claimed; but in view of the pioneer times in which he lived, and of the work accomplished by him, he must of necessity always command the highest respect of his countrymen. That he was a conscientious worker is proved by the fact that he travelled from one end of the country to the other to collect likenesses of the men he proposed to perpetuate on canvas. That he should have conceived the idea of perpetuating the events of the Revolution with his pencil gives evidence of a superior mind; that he should have undertaken such a task proves his courage; and that he should have accomplished it so successfully, under the most adverse circumstances, exhibits him as a man of rare perseverance.

A leading characteristic of this soldier-artist was his apparent sense of superiority over other men. It is true that he belonged to a family whose escutcheon had never been soiled by an unworthy act, and that he had for personal friends such men as Washington, Jefferson, John Adams, and Monroe; but he was in reality a lover of his fellow-men, and his seeming haughtiness was merely a physical peculiarity. Nor was it true that his dignity always militated against his influence. When, in 1777, the Continental Congress treated him with seeming *neglect* in not promptly sending him a commission for promotion, according to the advice of Gen. Gates, he returned the commission with a letter of explanation, in which he made this manly remark: "If I have committed any crime, or neglected any duty, since I engaged in the service of my country; if I have performed any action, or spoken a word in my public character, unworthy of my rank, — let me be tried by comrades, and broke: but I must not be thought so destitute of feeling as to bear degradation tamely." If that language proved him to be an aristocrat, the more of such people we have in public life the better. The special member of Congress who acted for him in this matter hastened to inform him that a mistake had been committed, and that his character was unblemished in the opinion of those who should have forwarded the commission. He also intimated that Col. Trumbull had better write another letter, and ask for his commission, &c. In his reply to this suggestion, he said, "I have never asked any office in the public service; nor will I ever. The very request would acknowledge and prove my unworthiness."

Col. Trumbull had a reputation for rudeness among artists: but it need not by any means follow that at heart he *was* rude; for artists are proverbially sensitive, and may have misjudged him. For instance: Col. Trumbull entered a young artist's studio one morning, and inquired, "Young man, how fast do you paint?" The answer was given. "And how much do you get for your portraits?" — "Only fifteen dollars, sir." — "And quite enough," observed the visitor; then added, "Young man, remember this: nine painters out of ten, great and small, err in drawing;" and went his way. It was an excellent piece of advice; but to this day that artist, who has painted portraits ever since, is an enemy of Col. Trumbull's. He told another young artist he had better be a shoemaker, and the artist now admits that he would probably have been richer to-day if he had. It was long a proverbial expression, originally credited to Col. Trumbull, that the framer makes more than the painter, indicating the spirit in which he intended the remark.

For thorough, old-school politeness and courtliness, Col. Trumbull had few equals. La Fayette, one of his most intimate friends, said that his works should be the first, if not the only, ornaments of his dwelling. Benjamin West, Charles James Fox, and Edmund Burke, were the men who interceded in his behalf, and had him released from his London prison. John Jay, Alexander Hamilton, Stephen Van Rensselaer, and men of that stamp, took pleasure in his companionship; and with David Hosack, DeWitt Clinton, and Robert R. Livingston, he was intimately associated in promoting a taste for the fine arts, and in conducting the affairs of the old American Academy. And, so far as the estimation in which he was held by the public generally both as a man and an artist is concerned, there is nothing that can speak more eloquently than the three hundred and forty-four names which were subscribed for a series of engravings from his paintings as far back as the year 1790. It is a royal list of names, which would never have been recorded in favor of a common man.

In the autumn of 1815 Col. Trumbull returned to America with his English wife, a lady of rare beauty. She died in 1825; and for nearly nineteen years, until his own death in 1843, he kept her portrait, which he had painted, closely veiled at the head of his bed. This portrait is now in possession of his niece, Miss Lanman of Norwich. The winter of 1819 he spent in Hartford at the house of Daniel Wadsworth, using the small tower upon the house as a studio, where he prepared some of his historical sketches. He was an elegant conversationalist, and, especially in his family, generous and gentle. As a colorist he was not equal to Stuart, nor could he rival Copley in drawing; but, in the higher attributes of art, many would say he excelled them both. Thackeray pronounced his work "the head of American art." Connecticut may well be proud that he was born upon her soil, that most of his best productions are in her possession, and that his remains are in her keeping. He died in 1843, retiring honorably from an eminence where many had jealously assailed him, — none less vindictively than the historian Dunlap, — but from which all together had not been able to shake him.

WILLIAM DUNLAP.

The great work of William Dunlap — his immortal work — was his "History of American Art." It is evident from his writings that he considered his paintings capable of making his name famous; but therein he was mistaken. Born in New Jersey in 1766 of poor parents, he made of himself what he very justly termed "a prodigy of unsuccessful success," spending a long life in the various capacities of artist, showman, lecturer, theatre-manager, play-writer, historian, and editor. Poor all his life, he would at the end have died in destitution, and been laid in an unvarnished coffin, but for friends in art and on the stage who sustained him and buried him by donations and benefits. In his ramblings as an artist, Mr. Dunlap passed some time in Connecticut, between New Haven and Hartford, and should justly be mentioned as one of the early influences for art in the State. It was during one of his many downfalls, early in 1812, that he first visited New Haven with the determination of making a fortune painting miniature portraits. A few friends upon whom he could depend gave him orders : but beyond that they began to drop off ; and soon sitters refused to take the miniatures, declaring they could not tell one from another. Mr. Dunlap was quick-tempered, as the proverbial old-school aristocratic gentleman always is ; and in six months he shook the dust of New Haven from his feet, denouncing the city as void of any art-feeling whatsoever. His book indirectly indicates that he never quite forgot this cold shoulder. He went to Boston, and took occasion to visit Stuart with some of the discarded portraits. It is said, that, in his inimitably quiet way, Stuart told him he thought the New-Haven people were right : "Brother Dunlap, it appears to me the good people of New Haven may have had some cause." Mr. Dunlap says that he advised him to return to New York, and study. He did return so far as Hartford in October, when he resolved to try the other capital. Whether it be complimentary to one or the other, or neither, he had much better success in the latter city, and remained for some time, with no regular studio except a small back-room behind the Rev. Joseph Stewart's museum. Evidently the reverend artist did not treat his brother Dunlap as circumspectly in all things as he supposed he deserved ; for the history speaks very disparagingly of the museum-keeper's art. He painted nothing but miniature portraits in the State ; and, shortly after his return to New York, he received an appointment in the paymaster's department, and entered government service.

ELKANAH TISDALE.

The artist Tisdale refused to give Mr. Dunlap any information regarding himself. Mr. Dunlap replies through his book, "The world will care nothing about it." Hence the world has lost what would to-day have been a valuable biography. When people learn that there is a pride that apes humility, the world will be much better off. A few (fortunately none of importance) have adopted the same course of reply to solicitations for the present volume, and the desire has been strong to treat them accordingly : but the unfortunate result of the course pursued above has prevented ; and facts thus refused have been sought for elsewhere, and invariably found, till, it is said with pride, no one will be able to discover by any internal evidence which were the few who refused.

In the case of Mr. Tisdale, every channel has been followed offering possible information; and a few facts have been gathered from the so-easily-forgotten yesterday. He was born in Lebanon, probably in the year 1771; though there is no record of his birth. He was the son of a wagon-maker, who, at the same time, was one of the old-time gentlemen; and the boy was brought up with all the dignity and refinement of aristocracy. It clung to him in a graceful polish through life. His first impressions of art were gathered from the lives and works of his illustrious townsmen, and his first knowledge in the carriage-shop. He had received no instruction whatever when he appeared in Hartford with a large painting, "The Battle of Lexington." Locally this was so popular, that it was almost immediately engraved; but Mr. Dunlap pronounces it "a very feeble affair." In the brief sketches that exist of Mr. Tisdale, he is referred to as "engraver and painter." Probably he understood engraving; but it was not the chief profession of his life, and indeed was virtually never his profession. The idea is derived from the fact that he was connected with the Hartford Graphic and Bank-Note Engraving Company; but his occupation was simply designing the vignettes. This gave him much time to pursue his art in other directions. He also designed many of the illustrations in the 1795 edition of Trumbull's "McFingal," and a political satire, entitled "Gerrymander," representing the famous Gerry in the shape of a serpent coiled suggestively about the State of Massachusetts. Tisdale's finest work by far was in miniature-portrait painting on ivory. One of these is now in possession of A. H. Emmons of Norwich, — a portrait of Gen. Knox, — fully displaying the touch of a master. The flesh-tints on the cheek, the fire in the eye, the waves of white hair, the life in the face of the florid old man, are remarkably fine.

Mr. Tisdale lived a bachelor, and lacked somewhat of the enthusiasm of necessity. He was short, fat, bald, and independent. It was probably the irresistible wave striking the immovable rock when he and Dunlap clashed. He was more given to thought than to painting, and very absent-minded. One morning a lad rapped on his door, calling for some ivory he had promised him on which to try his hand at miniature portraits. Hearing a lusty "Come in," he opened the door to find the fat artist in a bob-tailed shirt before a small mirror, shaving. Suddenly recollecting his position, he remarked, without lifting his razor, "I'm busy now, boy. Come again." The call was never repeated; for, a few days afterward, Mr. Tisdale left for Lebanon on business, not to return.

GIDEON FAIRMAN.

Gideon (more familiarly known as Colonel) Fairman was strictly an engraver, and as such must be omitted here ; but Col. Fairman, in a modest way, was also a painter. He was born in Newtown, Fairfield County, Conn., in June, 1774. His early inclinations led him toward the fine arts. His father, being in very moderate circumstances, was obliged to place him as apprentice to a blacksmith in New Milford. He spent his leisure time cutting figures in wood with his horseshoeing-knife. An itinerant engraver, seeing some of this work, earnestly urged his father to make the pathway to success easier before him. The engraver so far succeeded that the boy was placed under a silversmith, who was also an engraver. Having learned both trades, he connected himself with the National Bank-Note Engraving Company, where he was so successful, that for several years he lived in Philadelphia in luxurious style. Fraudulently relieved of his property and position, he turned to his first impulses, which had been toward painting. He produced a few pictures, which at once awakened public enthusiasm in his behalf ; and he resolved thereupon to be a painter. His work was bold, good in color, excellent in drawing. But another opportunity, offering more immediate returns in engraving, induced him to take up the graver again with the noble resolve to repay those who had suffered by his failure before indulging the longing of his life. This resolve, however, never found fulfilment. He was a portly, jovial man ; and the fierceness with which he devoted himself to the closely-confined life of the engraver was too much of a shock. He fell a victim to paralysis in 1827.

GOD BACCHUS.

At first thought, it may appear as overreaching the limits of the subject for the admission of an honorable dignitary to gather the above-named into the history of art in Connecticut. This charge may easily be substantiated, and as easily refuted. The argument, produced in a nutshell, amounts to this : While the god Bacchus is undoubtedly of Oriental birth and parentage, a comparatively late and remarkable edition of him owes existence wholly and entirely to art in Connecticut. This, enforced by the fact that his godship has exerted more influence over the State than any artist, and is himself fundamentally, superficially, and in common and uncommon acceptation, nothing more nor less than a child of art, clinches the nail, and renders an absolute necessity to the history of art in the State the biography of a god. Hence the following sketch of Bacchus, the revised edition of whom was born in Windham in the year we celebrated by the great centennial, 1776! He was fashioned by the hands of four members of his Britannic Majesty's naval service.

On the morning of the 10th of June, 1776, daring Puritans captured, in Long-Island Sound, the British ship "Bombrig." The blood-boiling details of the heroic fight and capture are irrelevant. The only relevancy in fact is, that four of the prisoners taken on that ship and morning were sent to the old Windham town-jail. Why they were sent there is as unaccount-

"BACCHUS." — FROM A PINE-LOG.

able as need be; for the rickety jail was only able to hold them for six months, and would not have succeeded so long, but that circumstances rendered it advisable for them to remain there of their own free will. In fact, as evidence of the frailty of its battlements and barriers, not only has it crumbled to dust in the hundred years that have passed, but even the site of it is altogether lost to memory. Probably the only relic of the days of that old jail is the god Bacchus.

These four men were respectively the commander, Edward Sneyd; the boatswain, John Coggin; a member of the carpenter's crew, John Russell; and an able-bodied seaman, William Cook. Sneyd was born in Kent County, Eng., in 1740. At fourteen he entered the royal naval service, and, after distinguished honors here and there, appeared in Long-Island Sound, commanding "The Bombrig," to which he was commissioned in 1775. Coggin was born in Killigan, county of Meath, Ireland, in 1731; entering the service at nineteen. He was on his way up the ladder when the Windham farmers chalked his feet. Russell, born in Hampshire, Eng., in 1749, began life in the capacity of a carpenter when twenty-three, and, serving a full apprenticeship, joined "The Bombrig" in 1775; and Cook was born in Great Yarmouth, Eng., 1794. He did not join the royal navy till he was thirty-one; which accounts for the limited progress he had made when checked in his march by the wooden walls of the Windham jail.

There was little fellow-sympathy for this quartet in the serious country-town, rasped and harrowed as it was by just such as they; and the durance into which they were thrown was no less vile on that account. There was one good soul, however, who took pity on them. The Widow Carey, as widows do, extended to them many tender-hearted tokens. The motives for her kindness and sympathy may not be explained at this late day, nor do they legitimately connect themselves with the question of art. Suffice it, that, whatever they were, the French leave which the four sailors took of the Windham jail and all appurtenances thereto, Widow Carey included, broke up any arrangements she may have made for the future. The fact, too, that she afterward appeared as Mrs. Fitch — the wife of the tavern-keeper, John Fitch, a true-born Yankee — is indicative of no seriously broken heart. Widow Carey was landlady of the tavern of Windham Green, and, in a somewhat sly but none the less open-hearted way, administered many well-directed favors. The imprisoned four took her delicacies both to stomach and to heart, and resolved between themselves upon a grateful acknowledgment. They were limited as to matter, and limited as to means; but pine was abundant thereabout, and they had four jack-knives between them. They obtained a huge log, and set themselves to work at the task of forming out of it a figure of Bacchus. This was a doubly appropriate gift to the Widow Carey; for she not only kept and tended bar, but had doubtless many a time, in her generous sympathy, contrived to smuggle a welcome draught to the parched prisoners.

The result of their labor is certainly artistic and clever. The jovial god of wine, naked and fat, sits astride a cask. On the cask in front of him rests a basket of fruit. One fat arm lovingly encircles the basket, and one fat hand is resting on the fruit. The great, round, dimpled, laughing face, with large eyes, and thick, wine-loving lips, has a peculiar expressiveness. In fact, the whole figure — time, place, and tools taken into consideration — is strangely life-like. In 1864, when it was upon a trip from New York to Hartford by cars, a lady, who caught sight of simply the upper half and the front of the figure, was with difficulty restrained from fainting. She thought "a man, even though he were a miserable dwarf, had no business to travel in a car with ladies, without clothes on." Grape-vine leaves cover the top of the head, and the hair beneath them is clusters of grapes. There are dimples in the cheeks and chin, a merry twinkle in the eyes, and a roguish smile on the parted lips, very becoming to the little fat god. The figure is painted a warm flesh-color. The eyes are black, the basket brown, the fruit of its various colors, the cask a dark red, and the hoops black; the work of the artist, George Bottume. The little god would stand twenty-six and a half inches high, and the keg is twenty-one inches long. The whole is of one solid piece, with the exception of five of the hoops. What a sermon might be preached upon this work, the notoriety it has given its authors, and the place in legendary history, when thousands of men performing deeds many-fold more wonderful are lost and forgotten before the first flower has blossomed on their graves!

The four prisoners completed the figure, presented it, and then made their escape. They reached Norwich, stole a small boat, and struck out for freedom. In "The Connecticut Gazette," published in New London, Friday, Nov. 29, 1776, is the following paragraph: "On Tuesday last one John Coggin, late boatswain of 'The Bombrig,' who, with three other prisoners, lately broke out of Windham jail, was found on board of a brig in this harbor. He gives the following account of said prisoners; viz.: The ʼght after breaking out of jail, they, with the help of one Lewis, who was ᵉn in a prize-vessel, stole a canoe near the Norwich landing, with which attempted to cross the sound to Long Island; but at the entrance of ᵉ, near Gull Island, the canoe overset, when all of them, except were drowned," &c.

ʼaint figure has outlived them by a century, and is as chubby smiling to-day as when first charmed from the pine-log, and the Windham jail. Many have been the vicissitudes through Time has turned the relic, sometimes nearly overturning side up again, better off, if any thing, for its tribulations, a hundred years to come.

ᶜe of the wine-god was as an ale-sign in front of the When the widow transferred herself to John Fitch, she transferred the Bacchus to the front of the Fitch Tavern. By the heirs of Fitch it was sold to Lucius Abbee, landlord of the Stamford House, who balanced the cask and its rider on the limb of a huge elm in front of his door. While on that lofty seat it passed into the hands of Zaphney Curtis; but it never moved from the elm-tree till the September gale of 1856 left it on the ground with an arm broken off, and otherwise bruised. Bacchus, regardless of his dignity and good-will, was carried into the wood-shed, and left there half buried in dust and kindlings, which fate seemed to destine him to become a part of. Fortunately William Cummings discovered the merry god in his desolation, and bought him for twenty-five cents. Then came better days for Bacchus.

He was purchased from Mr. Cummings in 1859, who had secured complete repairs and a thorough renovation. In 1864 it went to New York, and was brought to Hartford in 1872, where it has since remained.

No more weather-beating awaits the round, dimpled relic. It is carefully housed and protected, and properly valued. A hundred years circle that rimless crown. A hundred years have wound a weary way before the great black eyes. It is nothing but a comical wooden image on a small wooden cask, but something sublime after all, something inspiring respect, something possessing a vast amount of dignity. And thus the little god Bacchus is laid aside again to sit at ease astride his cask, and clasp and fondle the grapes in his basket.

EDWARD G. MALBONE.

With no intention of robbing Rhode Island of her famous Malbone, born in Newport, 1777, it is yet necessary to explain a certain strong influence for art, and especially miniature-portrait painting, noticeable at the beginning of the nineteenth century, to say that the great painter honored the State with his presence. The only pictures now in known possession that were painted during this time are those of a family named Woodbridge, and indicate that they were painted about 1798 or 1799. It could not well have been earlier; and in 1800 the artist went abroad, when his style materially changed.

JOHN COLES.

A fellow-student under Gilbert Stuart with Frothingham, and a life-friend of that artist, John Coles by name, born 1780, came into possession of a farm in Durham, Conn., in 1831, and established himself in a studio in Hartford, in a building, long since demolished, that stood upon the corner of Main and Asylum Streets. Three years he spent continually in Hartford. Thereafter, for fifteen years, he spent the summers on his farm, and winters in Hartford, moving to Providence in 1849, and to Worcester, Mass., a short time later. In 1832 Mr. Frothingham spoke of him as the finest portrait-painter of America. This, however, appears something like the prejudice of mutual admiration; for Mr. Coles many times referred to Frothingham as second only to Stuart, his master. Coles was a remarkably handsome man in figure and in face, except for a light marking of small-pox. His excellent figure, dark hair and eyes, and characteristically sad expression, induced Mr. Stuart to secure him as the model for Daniel in his "Nebuchadnezzar's Feast." It is said to be an excellent likeness. He was a fatalist, and, as a principle of his life, devoted two hours every day to reading such works as Newton's and Robert Dale Owen's. His work was good in every sense. He had carefully mastered the laws; but it excelled in nothing, having no warmth of romance or fancy. He was too matter-of-fact, and so was his work. Naturally an elegant conversationalist, his whole life was chilled by his morbid thoughts. Naturally possessing the qualities of a brilliant artist, his work was subdued and cold under the same influence. The most of his work was in bust-portrait, twenty-two by twenty-seven inches. He always painted upon panel, with a lead-colored background. His chief perfection was in drawing and modelling; and, in all, much of his work was very fine. It is most remarkable, that, especially with such a friend as James Frothingham possessing so high an opinion of him, John Coles has never received the attention of any historian or writer whatsoever.

ANSON DICKINSON.

One of the early miniature-portrait painters of Connecticut was Anson Dickinson, born in Litchfield, Conn., 1780. His choice of profession was that of the silversmith. He was a man of genius, and at twenty years began painting, with no more instruction than the inspection of some of Malbone's work which he had done in the State a year previous. His early struggles in art were few. His talent easily overcame all obstacles. In 1811 the best critics of America pronounced him the first miniature-portrait painter in New-York City; but he was too handsome for his own safety. Narcissus-like, waylaid by his own beauty, he finally merited in some degree the condemnation which Mr. Dunlap pronounced upon him, — that he was without credit either to art or to himself; yet he was a remarkably fine artist. In 1818 he went to Canada, married a French-Canadian, painted in Northern New England, and in 1840 returned to Connecticut, settled in New Haven, where he painted for five years; then moved to Hartford, where he painted until he died late in 1847. His color was excellent, his drawing (according to common exaggeration) perfect. His chief fault was, that in endeavoring to imitate Malbone, who had inspired him to art, he followed so closely, that, without that painter's power, many of his pictures have a thin, washy appearance. He was a man of great personal energy and assurance.

GEORGE MUNGER.

Another miniature-portrait painter of the early days of art in the State was George Munger, born in Guilford in 1783. He was a relative of Anson Dickinson, and they began study together in New Haven; but a severe attack of small-pox interrupted Mr. Munger's plans, and he gave up the work for eleven years. In 1815 he again found himself able to take up the brush. He threw the pent enthusiasm of all the years of silence into it, and worked with such vehemence, that to-day his miniatures are honored where his cousin's are almost forgotten. Personally he was mild and gentle, but immovably determined. Mr. Jocelyn of New Haven has a miniature by Munger, of delicate touch and excellent color, showing a masterly handling. He expended every spark of vitality upon his art, and, in his weakened condition, did not physically sustain himself. He died in 1824, having lived two lives in one in the last eight years. He left two daughters artistically inclined, who are mentioned elsewhere.

SAMUEL WALDO.

One of the best-known artists through the medium of history is Samuel Waldo, portrait-painter, born in Windham, Conn., 1783. His first education in art was gathered from the Rev. Joseph Stewart in the old Museum Hall. He began his practice of art in Litchfield, and, having laid up a convenient sum in an incredibly short time, went to New York for a year of study; then sailed for London, where he was received as a pupil of Benjamin West, and studied for three years. Returning, he spent his life in painting in New York and Hartford; and died Feb. 16, 1861.

In Hartford his studio was in Exchange Corner. His invariable politeness and dignity secured for him a large circle of friends, and abundant orders every time he came to the city; which rendered his visits fortunately frequent, and often of considerable length. It may not be said that in any one particular his work excels that of other artists; but he stood above most in his day as the result of untiring faithfulness to every detail. This corresponds with the first advice he gave his pupil and final partner, Jewett: "When you paint a coat-sleeve, paint it as carefully as you paint an eye." When death claimed him, at the age of seventy-eight, he was still before his easel, and left a copy of one of Stuart's pictures half finished, which he was making on an order. One of his best paintings is a bust-portrait of himself in the National Academy. Another excellent portrait is a three-quarter length of the artist Henry C. Shumway in his official uniform. The flesh-tints are especially admirable, and even the silver belt-plate is a valuable study in itself. Mr. Waldo was one of the best art-critics of his day; bold and fearless in his judgment, but universally respected for his kind-hearted generosity. His work is perhaps better known under the firm-name of Waldo & Jewett. A sketch of Mr. Jewett is inserted later.

GEORGE FREEMAN.

Among the names unfortunately forgotten by historians is that of George Freeman, born at Spring Hill, near Mansfield Centre, Conn., April 21, 1789. He was a painter of miniature portraits on porcelain and ivory, and of no small repute either in England or America. His father was a farmer of very moderate means, and all that he was in later years resulted from his own personal efforts. Of the earlier pictures of his painting that remain are one of Mrs. Sigourney, and several in possession of Mrs. H. B. Beach of Hartford, executed about 1810. In 1813 he went abroad, remaining in Europe twenty-four years; which accounts for Mr. Dunlap's oversight. He returned without warning, and took dinner with his father, telling him he had met his son in London, without being recognized. While abroad, he studied in Paris and London. In the latter city his work was highly praised, and he received the distinguished honor of being allowed to paint Queen Victoria and Prince Albert from life. He died in Hartford March 7, 1868.

GEORGE FRANCIS.

Long and well known for other good qualities, George Francis also possessed a taste and talent for art, that, though hidden under a bushel, was yet enough before the public to identify his name with the art of the State. He was born in Hartford in 1790, and died there 1873. He studied drawing under Benjamin West, and coloring with Washington Allston; but his father left a large business in carriage-making in such a way that his son was literally obliged to take it up. Thereafter art ceased to be a profession; but to the end of his life it was an entertaining pastime. At the end of the shop he had enclosed a small studio, where he designed the ornamental work for sleighs and carriages, and occasionally painted a portrait or a landscape. Never having known in art the sweet hand that brought bread to a hungry family, or the lovely goddess saying to the patient plodder, "Friend, go up higher," he failed, of course, in the pure devotion that must be a part of the successful artist; but his pictures have a decided merit, and much artistic skill. In the effect of light and shade he was particularly successful. Mr. Francis was a genial, social man, an active member of the first temperance society, and a man thoroughly respected. It was a boast of his later years, that he had never been sick for a day in his life. This was strangely carried to the end; and when eighty-three, in perfect health, he was stricken with a paralytic shock, from which he never regained consciousness.

His grand-daughter Miss Fannie Francis, now studying at Wellesley, seems to have gathered up his mantle. She has already painted several landscape-scenes that in drawing are very good, and in color promise much for the future.

HEZEKIAH AUGUR.

The first Connecticut sculptor was Hezekiah Augur, born in New Haven, February, 1791, the son of a carpenter. Augur, as a boy, enjoyed his father's trade: he enjoyed it more than his father did. At eight years old he "preferred the confines of the shop to fighting schoolfellows," to quote from a letter of his writing. This mildness of temper was to some extent unfortunate, preventing him from fighting his way into art till over thirty-four years old; though from childhood he was an artist. He had better have left carving wood with his father's tools now and then, and gone out and fought his schoolfellows. The experience would have been good for him.

His father did not like this carving and cutting, having that objection to his own business so common to the paternal mind. He put the boy under a grocer, when nine years old, to "learn a trade." Hezekiah did learn a trade. The grocer could make and mend shoes; and, counting it better to be a doorkeeper in art than a nabob in merchandise, Hezekiah applied himself to the awl. When the time for which he was bound expired, he issued an abominably poor grocer, but a proficient cobbler. Shoemaking was not in his father's programme for his son. He presented him with two thousand dollars and a position in a firm of reputedly honorable men as partner in the dry-goods business. This was a mistake on the part of all concerned. It was the great blunder of Hezekiah Augur's life. He knew his desires and ambition; and instead of passing unobjectingly, as he admits, into one plan or another, he should have asserted himself, and let Art claim her own. His partnership continued but three years; when, he never knew precisely how, it was demonstrated to him that his two thousand dollars were not only disposed of, but that he stood indebted to the rest of the firm to the amount of seven thousand dollars more. By nature keenly sensitive, the sudden fall, after having lived upon the most social terms in the best society of New Haven, was a bitter blow, from which he did not easily recover. He found the truth of the old adage, that wealth makes honorable men at a cost of much suffering; and, wholly dropped and forgotten by his old associates, he opened a little fruit-stand, where, in a sense, he succeeded. Here he reverted to deserted art again, and carved elaborately a mahogany case for a musical instrument which he had made. It was only by chance that this ever saw the light. After keeping it for some time in secret, he took it to a cabinet-maker to varnish. The fine workmanship displayed secured him work and good pay, carving the legs of mahogany chairs and ornaments for two years. At the end of that time, having saved a considerable sum, he committed another blunder in paying up as much as he could of his indebtedness to the dry-goods firm. Encouraged by this, they began a system of dunning, that so alarmed Mr. Augur, that he sold out his fruit-stand and carving business. The short, thin man, with light-brown hair, an exceptionally fair, almost florid complexion, who was forever carving behind the counter, was missed from the fruit-stand; but the general opinion among his former friends was that it was only another failure, for which the first had made him famous.

In the seclusion into which his sensitiveness and timidity forced him he completed an invention for making worsted lace, which brought him a large price, and at once enabled him to free himself from debt. At almost the same time his father died: and, all constraint being removed at the eleventh hour, he turned his whole soul toward art; though he said for himself of this final devotion, "With a life-blot behind me, my only ambition is to drown memory and reflection in a pleasant pastime." In 1847 he also brought out a carving-machine, which is still used in several factories for carving piano-legs. He originated many inventions in the course of his life; one of the more prominent being one rarely credited to him, — that of producing the first bracket-saw.

He carved so finely in wood, that Professor Morse urged him to attempt a work in marble. His first endeavor was upon the head of Apollo. He went at his marble, as he had his wood, with no more of a model than his own fancy furnished him. This, of course, necessitated exceedingly slow work, and increased the timidity of expression; but the result was exciting and encouraging. He then produced a head of Washington and a figure of Sappho; and his fame was secure, so far as purely native talent, with no education whatever, could win it.

He did some work on orders from New Haven and Hartford; but his skill, though so remarkable, was not such as was calculated to yield a large income, except as works of his fancy might sell. On an order from Congress, he made a bust of Chief Justice Ellsworth, that now stands in the Supreme-Court room in Washington.

Mr. Augur's great work, and one that merits all the fame it achieved for its author, is the often-quoted pair of marble statuettes, "Jephthah and his Daughter." The remarkable feature, of course, is that they are carved without model. But in themselves, though expressing the faults natural to such a course, they possess much that is indicative of an exceptionally high rank of ability. In each the expression of face and limb, and the characteristic unity throughout, are worthy of great commendation. The head of the "Daughter" is particularly fine in the arrangement of the hair. He invited Washington Allston to criticise the work. Relating the fact to a friend, he said, "Mr. Allston walked about them for thirty minutes without speaking, and the perspiration poured from me like rain during the whole half-hour."

Both in character and ability he was a man well fitted to hold a much higher position than circumstances ever allowed him to occupy. In 1833 he was made an honorary member of the alumni of Yale College. He died in January, 1858, with much, yet little, left behind as the result of his life's labor.

GEORGIO CARDELLI.

There was an Italian, Georgio Cardelli, born in Florence in 1791, who there learned the double profession of sculpture and painting, who came to New York in 1816. His patronage was not extensive at the first; but in a year he received the distinguished honor of an order from Mr. Trumbull for a bust of himself and Mrs. Trumbull. The casts were prepared; but, finding fault with them, Mr. Trumbull refused to take them. The sculptor became excited. Mr. Trumbull in turn remarked, "But you cannot be a popular sculptor in New York if I refuse to indorse you." Thereupon Cardelli declared he would no longer be a sculptor of New York at all; and, leaving his sculptor's tools, he took brush and easel, as of easier transportation, and became an itinerant. Hartford received two visits from Cardelli, in each of which he professedly settled down for life, but eventually moved on. It was 1820 when he first appeared, and Italy-educated artists were not so plenty that they could be despised. He received orders, and became very popular among the first families of the city. Among those of his works remaining in the city, one is in possession of the family of the late Ezra Clark, and óne in the Wadsworth Gallery. They are hard, lifeless pictures, thoroughly Florentine, but said to be excellent likenesses. Georgio Cardelli was not a man to be trifled with. Those in the city who remember him as a gloomy cloud over their childhood recall with a shudder a lowering, black-eyed, long black-haired, wrinkled, highly excitable savage, whom none of them dared look at except from behind a chair, and their fathers dare not criticise for love of their lives.

SAMUEL FINLEY BREESE MORSE.

Massachusetts glories in producing one of the greatest men ever born on the free soil of America. It was at the foot of Breed's Hill, April, 1791, — whither the reverend geographer and philosopher, Jedediah Morse, D.D., had moved, to accept a pastorate, from Woodstock, Conn., — that Samuel F. B. Morse was born. As all of the ancestors of Professor Morse

SAMUEL F. B. MORSE.

for ages were wisely and well honored citizens of Connecticut, as his education was gained in the State, and as nearly all of his art-life spent in America passed while his home was in Connecticut, it may not appear like robbing another State to claim the honor of recognizing among the artists of Connecticut the very great artist, Samuel F. B. Morse.

His predilections in favor of art were early and strongly expressed. When but four years old, he was caught in the act of caricaturing his schoolmistress with a pin on a case of drawers. He was born of a race of thinkers; and this trait, too, was early developed in the lad, who at fourteen passed the examination successfully, entering Yale College. For domestic reasons, his father saw fit to withhold him a year; so that he entered with the class in 1807, when he passed honorably through four years of study, partially supporting himself in the course of it by painting portraits. He received for these crude specimens of purely native ability, in the shape of miniatures on ivory, five dollars each, the sitter furnishing his own ivory; and for a profile-drawing one dollar, which, he says in a letter, very many of the students afforded. He was of Puritanical ancestry; and this was evident throughout his life in a character of spotless purity, integrity, and nobility.

On graduating, the grave question of the future was presented in all its solemnity by his forethoughtful father, and received the response, "I think I am cut out for a painter." Dr. Morse was no man to make light of a sober thought, and at once proceeded, in his energetic way, to place at his son's command every facility. The result was six months' study in America under Washington Allston, and four successive years of study and intimacy with him immediately thereafter in England. Among his first accomplishments of note and celebrity was his "Dying Hercules." The original clay model and the large oil-painting from it are in the Yale Art Building. It was undertaken at the suggestion of his master Allston, who often modelled before he painted, and was at first perfected in but one view, — that required for his painting. The work was so admirably done, that Allston insisted upon his completing it. It received the gold medal for superiority in original modelling in England, though the war of 1812 was at its height. Returning, Mr. Morse made several unsatisfactory endeavors to establish himself as an historical painter. He accepted the inevitable, and for support became a portrait-painter. He married a lady of inestimable sweetness and moral worth, and in 1820 moved with his own and his father's family to New Haven. Through the greater part of the fall and the early winter of 1821 he painted portraits in Hartford, receiving only fifteen dollars apiece for them; but determined to do "even that, or more, sooner than fall into debt." In the winter of 1821 he was working upon his much-abused and exceedingly fine picture of "The House and Senate at Washington," at which, as an evidence of the nature of the man, he worked for sixteen hours a day, and so enthusiastically, that once he got up at midnight, after an hour's sleep, prepared himself for work, and attempted to paint before he discovered that it was moonlight, and not sunrise; and at another time attempted to enter the hall to begin sketching on Sunday, having forgotten the calendar.

In 1822, while painting in New Haven, Mr. Morse presented the Yale-College Library with five hundred dollars. This was, perhaps, the most munificent gift ever contributed, when the circumstances are considered; for, not six months later, when a hall-thief stole the artist's hat, he wrote, that, to buy another, he was obliged to break the last five-dollar bill he possessed, and had no knowledge of where the next was coming from. In his later prosperity he exhibited the same generosity in presenting to the

"THE SISTERS." — BY S. F. B. MORSE.

art-gallery of the college a painting of Allston's for which he paid seven thousand dollars. In 1824 he was appointed upon the Mexican Commission, and left for Washington in high hopes of receiving great profit from such a trip. On reaching Washington he learned that the commission had been abandoned. The following winter better times appeared on the horizon in a government order for a portrait of Gen. LaFayette. He went again to Washington, and had secured two sittings, when news reached him of the sudden death of his wife, to whom he was bound heart and life.

The house in which Mr. Morse lived while in New Haven was a low-roofed cottage, nearly upon the site of the present Yale Art Building.

The appearance of the artist was very different from that of the inventor of the telegraph system. His hair was short, and his face smooth-shaven; but the character of the schoolboy, the collegiate, the art-student, the painter, the writer, the chemist, the lecturer, the inventor of the engine, the master of the telegraph, was one and the same throughout, — the exemplification of every thing that makes the noble, honorable man.

Several of the artist's finest works are owned in Connecticut. That of Mrs. D. C. DeForest, which now hangs in the Yale Art Building, has one of the most perfect hands ever put upon canvas. The face also is soft, sweet, and wonderfully life-like. Two portraits, that are among his remarkable productions, have fortunately come into possession of the Hartford Historical Society through the generosity of Walter Chester, Esq., of New York. They are portraits of Judge Mitchell and his wife. The family were anxious to secure the portrait of the judge; but the old gentleman stubbornly refused. Mrs. Mitchell set herself to the task of outwitting her lord, and was victorious. Mr. Morse was engaged to paint her portrait. The judge readily complied with that request. Mr. Morse was invited to board at the house while painting, and, when the work was done, received his pay for two oil-paintings instead of one. The faces are both admirable, heavily painted, with fine effect. They show the difference in the mode of work, the judge's face being somewhat more constrained. They are low in tone, warm in color, living, thinking portraits. The judge evidently belonged to the snuff-takers, and his mouth is pursed as though half smiling under the effects of an after-dinner snuff. The lady's face combines the sweetest graces of nature and art. The merry eye is wreathed with the wrinkles of age. The oval but wrinkled cheeks are surrounded with a finely painted lace cap, and the lace puffs about the neck and over the bosom display a proficiency rarely attained. The painting by Morse lately presented to the Lenox Gallery by Mr. Osborne of New York was found at an auction, and bought against competitors who were absolutely ignorant of what they were bidding for; which accounts for the very low price paid for it by Mr. Osborne. Professor Morse had also a rare gift in his power of clothing his thoughts with words in exceptionally fine poetry. "The Serenade," published in "The Talisman" while he was in New Haven, was a beautiful composition both written and illustrated by himself.

When the present Emperor of Brazil visited the Yale Art Building he was particularly interested in the works of Professor Morse, and, receiving a gift of his portrait, pressed it to his heart, exclaiming in English, "I shall *conserve* this." Professor Morse was not always the meek man commonly appearing. The scar in his forehead was the mark of a British soldier's bayonet, received while he was waiting in a dense throng to see the " United Sovereigns " pass.   Mr. Morse was not politically prepossessed in favor of the British at the time, and instantly grappled with the soldier. He was fortunately dragged away by friends in the crowd before his name was learned.   He was an earnest patriot, and at times, during the war of 1812, was unable to work for days together.   The same enthusiasm, though not always obvious, marked every action of his life.   In art Mr. Morse was essentially a colorist.   His work is doubtless very uneven ; but the best indicates the man, while the poorest but signifies that still grander thoughts were drawing his mind from the canvas.

ALVIN FISHER.

Born in Needham in 1792, Alvin Fisher, when twenty-four years old, began portrait-painting on an education gained chiefly from observation. After a year he gave up portraits for farm-scenes, in which he was very successful.   In 1820 he returned to portrait-painting, and thereafter combined the two.   In 1822 Mr. Fisher established himself in Hartford.   His work was chiefly pastoral, that class of paintings being almost a novelty in the State.   Among his more important works was one of Niagara Falls, which was engraved by Asaph Willard.   He painted in Hartford for three years, and, as the first pastoral painter of importance to visit the State, produced an impression and influence visible afterward.   He left for an extended trip and study in Europe, and, returning, settled in Boston.   He died at Dedham Feb. 14, 1863.

GEORGE CATLIN.

One of the large family of Catlins emanating from Litchfield, Conn., George Catlin, born in Wyoming Valley, Penn., 1793, returned to his father's home to study law.   He was admitted to the bar in Litchfield, and that closed his legal career.   He went to West Point ; when, after establishing the foundation for a military life, he moved to Philadelphia, and at once devoted himself, life and limb, to the acquirement of a thorough knowledge of art.   As a profession he carried art a little beyond his former studies, into a very moderate use.   He had a studio in Hartford for a short time in 1824.   Ex-Gov. Catlin of Hartford has a portrait of his father painted by the artist in Litchfield, expressive of perfect composure and knowledge of art, and of no small amount of ability, but lacking in warmth and delicacy.   Leaving Hartford, Mr. Catlin moved his studio to New York, and, May 3, 1825, was elected to the National Academy.   The most important order which Mr. Catlin received was from the State of New York, through Mrs. Clinton, for a portrait of Gov. DeWitt Clinton. Professor Morse had painted a portrait of the governor when in one of his absent-minded moods, and made an utter failure of it. Mr. Catlin was a friend of the family; and, when the portrait was to be painted for the City Hall, Mrs. Clinton insisted that Catlin should paint it: unfortunately this resulted in one of the poorest portraits in the governor's room. For the spring exhibition of 1826 he painted Mrs. Clinton's portrait and several others. His pictures did not receive the attention he supposed they deserved; and he indignantly withdrew them, and sent in his resignation as an academician, which was accepted May 3, 1826. Action in his pictures is generally well expressed, the effect is good, but the modelling is always seriously defective. In 1832 Mr. Catlin started upon his trip among the Indians, which made him famous in both America and Europe, through the almost endless use he made of it, as well as of a trip of exploration in Africa, laying up resources which profited him afterward in the lecture-field, in books, in exhibitions, in galleries of sketches, in cabinets of curiosities, and many other ways. In 1842 he moved to London, where, as an elegant conversationalist, a brilliant writer, overflowing with wit, anecdote, and information, he was much admired and sought after. In 1874 he exhibited and sold at auction his entire collection of Indian sketches and relics; and a year after, a white-haired, very deaf old man came to the close of his eventful life as a lawyer, a soldier, an artist, a showman, an explorer, a lecturer, an historian, and a tourist, that, after all, through its own versatility failed to register in any way proportionate with itself.

EDWIN PERCIVAL.

A brother of the poet Percival, and James G. Percival the actor, Edwin Percival, fully as eccentric and possibly as gifted as either, was born in Kensington, Conn., 1793. In 1830 he came to Hartford to study art; assigning no reason for this sudden determination, but evincing much taste and considerable talent. Three years later he went to Albany in partnership with Henry Bryant. His drawing was always good, and in color his pictures are pleasing. He excelled in ideal sketches. "Three Daughters of Job" was the best work that came from his easel, and gained for him, very justly, an enviable local reputation. He was a man of excellent education and culture, but subject to attacks of the most depressing melancholy. He went from Albany to Troy, N.Y., and there, under the influence of one of these despondencies, resolved that he would eat nothing more. He literally starved to death.

WILLIAM JEWETT.

The pupil and partner of Samuel Waldo, William Jewett, was born in East Haddam, Conn., Feb. 14, 1795. The doorway through which he entered art was the proverbial carriage-shop. After serving his apprenticeship there, Mr. Waldo engaged him to grind colors, and, being pleased with the lad, took him into his family. The young student worked so thoroughly into his master's manner, that in time a partnership was formed, in which both worked upon the same picture, and only the most experienced could detect the individual work of either. As Mr. Jewett did very little single-handed work, it is impossible to form any distinct criticism. That he satisfied so critical an artist as Samuel Waldo is evidence sufficient of his ability. He was a quiet, retiring man, with little to say, and better satisfied to be alone than in society.

DANIEL DICKINSON,

a younger brother of Anson Dickinson, was born in Litchfield, Conn., in 1795. In 1812, Daniel Dickinson, following the path of his brother, went to New Haven to study art. Finding no favorable opening, but meeting with Mr. Jocelyn, who was then studying drawing by himself, he adopted the same method. He was almost unconsciously drawn into miniature-portrait painting; and the leisure time of his experimental years in art was devoted to fancy sketches, many of which were very attractive and popular. This work consisted chiefly in arranging the female figure in every conceivable graceful attitude: some of the sketches possessed much artistic merit. In 1830 he moved his studio to Philadelphia, and began the study of oil-painting. In this he was so successful and well patronized, that he remained through a long life in that city. He has never received historical notice, as can be discovered, though, in point of ability, not far inferior to his brother.

NATHANIEL JOCELYN.

The patriarch of American art (being to-day the oldest native artist of notoriety living), Nathaniel Jocelyn, is still actively engaged in his studio in New Haven, where he was born Jan. 31, 1796, six months before his next fellow-laborer, Ashur B. Durand. As with Mr. Durand, his father was a watchmaker; and the boy was fed upon the understanding, that, in the common course of things, he was to follow him. His early inclinations toward the creative art were easily satisfied with this prospect; and, when twelve years old, his father boasted of him that he knew every wheel and screw in the best watch in the country. Wheels and screws, however, did not long satisfy the measure of the young man's ambition. When only fifteen, he began, with himself as instructor, a thorough course of study in drawing, and three years later apprenticed himself to an engraver. When twenty-one, he entered into partnership with Tisdale, Dantforth, & Willard, in the Hartford Graphic and Bank-Note Engraving Company, and later, with Mr. Dantforth, virtually founded the National Bank-Note Engraving Company. The work that fell to him in this was the lettering, which did not please him; and in 1820 he gave up engraving, changing the graver for the pencil, with which he started at once for Savannah, Ga., as a portrait-painter. The spirit which prompted and the courage which

NATHANIEL JOCELYN.

accomplished this bold step are worthy accessories to a successful career. He remained but a short time at the South, returning much benefited by the experience, to establish himself in New Haven. An enthusiastic spirit tempted him beyond the confines of art into large real-estate transactions, — laying out streets, and inaugurating many improvements that are the pride of New Haven to-day. For a time he continued before his easel, and to the first exhibition of the National Academy, on Reade Street and Broadway, 1826, sent several portraits which Mr. Dunlap pronounced unqualifiedly meritorious. But he gradually became so deeply drawn into his ventures, that he left his studio entirely; and in the crisis of 1843 he was ingulfed. However uncomfortable, this was a fortunate thing for his art; for it drove him again to his easel for support. In 1829 he went abroad chiefly upon matters of other business. Aided, however, by a ready perception of opportunity that has characterized his life, he formed many valuable acquaintances, and gained much information in matters of art. He travelled southward from London with Professor Morse, entering Paris with him on New-Year's Day, 1830.

"CINQUE."—FROM LIFE, BY NATHANIEL JOCELYN.

In 1834 Mr. Dunlap said of the artist's apartments, "He is established in the most eligible suite of rooms for painting and exhibiting that I know of." In 1849 this elegant studio was destroyed by fire; and almost the only thing of value saved was a black-wood easel on which Col. Trumbull painted, which Mr. Jocelyn still preserves. After the fire the artist moved to New York. He had long been an honorary member of the National Academy, and now they elected him an academician. He returned to New Haven, however, before the year was gone in which he was to have made good his election ; and, as it appeared his intention to remain there, the society over-jealously rescinded the vote.   Mr. Jocelyn was also elected honorary member of the Philadelphia Art Union ; but, the presentation being made directly after an action on the part of the Union which had aroused the artist's strong antislavery sentiments, he declined it without limitation.   He also received the gold palette for the best portrait exhibited in the State in 1844.   Col. Trumbull pronounced his head of Judge Lanman, which is now owned by Judge L. Foster, an excellent specimen of portraiture.   Several of the artist's best portraits hang in the Yale Art Gallery, displaying a strength of touch, grace of modelling, and refined taste, justly supporting him in the position he has attained.   As a teacher, he has had among his pupils many celebrated artists.   As a supporter of the fine arts, he is as genial, unaffected, and enthusiastic to-day as ever in his life.

LUCIUS MUNSON.

To a very short career in art Lucius Munson was born in New Haven, Dec. 15, 1796.   When eighteen he had no thought of making art a profession, or even a pastime.   He was an easy, off-hand draughtsman, but with a small sum of money accumulated was on the point of buying a farm on which to spend his life, when Mr. Jocelyn persuaded him to test his artistic ability.   The passion of the artist seemed suddenly to spring upon him.   He gave up every thing to study portrait-painting.   At the end of a year, realizing the need of a more thorough education, he went to New York, and studied drawing in the National Academy till 1818.   He practised his art for a year in New Haven ; then went to South Carolina, where orders were received in such abundance, that his health gave way in filling them.   He returned to New Haven for a year, when he was obliged to seek a warmer climate.   He went to Bermuda, and the following summer to Turk's Island, where he died suddenly on the 27th of July, 1823.   An inordinate ambition to accumulate enough to study art in Europe continually drove him beyond his strength.   As a portrait-painter he not only gave good promise for the future, but had already accomplished much.   His pictures show good taste and skill in drawing. He was a careful student, and his work was free and bold.   The public were pleased with the likenesses he obtained ; but, ignorant of the method by which the effects were produced, popularly called him "a remarkable dauber," — a greater compliment, after all, than they supposed.

S. S. OSGOOD.

Mr. S. S. Osgood is said to have been born in New Haven, 1798. These facts are probably correct, but are given on the strength of a single statement for which confirmation or contradiction is wanting. Hence they should not be too implicitly relied upon. When a child, he was taken to Boston. There, after the usual vicissitudes, he was at last given up to art, and studied for five years ; when, in 1825, he returned to Connecticut, and opened a studio in the old Eagle Hotel, on Main Street, Hartford. He remained for five years, and, being the principal portrait-painter in the city at the time, received large orders and obtained good prices, though his work was crude and unsatisfactory compared with that which he performed later in life. In 1830 he married Frances Sargent Lock, the poetess. They sailed at once for Europe. There Mr. Osgood entered upon a course of study which resulted in making him one of the finest portrait-painters of the day. In England he painted the portraits of Lord Lyndhurst, Mrs. Norton, and others, with success that gave him a wide reputation. He returned to his studio in Hartford in 1842, and painted, among those of other prominent men, an admirable portrait of Gov. Catlin. He painted slowly ; but his pictures have both ease and strength. The late James B. Hosmer had a fine painting of a dog which Mr. Osgood presented him, though animal-painting was apparently something to which he devoted little or no attention. Shortly after returning to Hartford, he was greatly afflicted in the death of his wife and two daughters. He was urged to go to Europe to shake off the melancholy. "Nonsense!" he replied. "Can a man leave himself here, and go abroad ? " Subsequently, however, he went to California, where he rapidly gathered a large fortune.

ISAAC SHEFFIELD.

An artist named Isaac Sheffield has left a limited number of portraits and figure-pieces about New London. He says, in a letter that has come to light, "I came here from my home in Guilford when thirty-five." This is the only clew that has been discovered, and, together with the fact that his earliest pictures are dated 1833, leads to the impression that he was born in Guilford, 1798. The portraits are all red-faced, and most of them sea-captains, with one single telescope in the hand of every one, while they all stand before a red curtain. Otherwise there is not much that is noteworthy. The artist died in 1845.

BENJAMIN HUTCHINS COE.

The drawing-teacher of wide fame, Benjamin H. Coe, was born in Hartford, Conn., Oct. 8, 1799. His pictures are quiet, pleasant views; but his merit lay in his teaching. F. E. Church and E. S. Bartholomew, beside many others, came to him for their first information. He lived as a farmer, till, as he said of himself, he was too old to learn more than the rudiments. Always having possessed a great fondness for art, he mastered these rudiments with wonderful activity and success. He possessed a remarkable faculty for imparting truths in a way to fasten them in memory; and a long life of teaching both private students and large classes in nearly

BENJAMIN HUTCHINS COE.

all of the important cities of New England, New York, and New Jersey, sustains this reputation. He had a very large private school in the University Building, in New-York City; moving from there in 1854 to his present home in New Haven. He opened his last school there, which he carried on successfully for ten years; then gave it up to one of his pupils, and entered into the temperance-work, writing and distributing tracts, and working in ale-houses, with the vigor of a young convert. Within a year, failing health has somewhat interrupted this work.

FRANCIS ALEXANDER.

Mr. Dunlap gives a very complete history of the early life of Francis Alexander. He was born in Killingly, Windham County, Conn., in February, 1800. His father was a poor farmer. His first inspiration toward art was a desire to copy some fish he had caught, which he did in water-color. His early life was inartistic. He wrote to Mr. Dunlap, " I used to go three miles before sunrise, and reap all day for a bushel of rye." A lad who from these circumstances could enter the field of art at all must be acknowledged to possess certain very desirable qualities. His first trip to New York, for the purpose of studying art, he made in September as deck-passenger on a steamboat from Norwich. Mrs. Gen. James B. Mason of Providence saw two of his paintings, and fortunately resolved to bring the young artist out. He remained two years in Providence,.progressing rapidly ; then went to Boston, where he was welcomed by Gilbert Stuart, and well recommended by Col. Trumbull. Francis Alexander was contemporary with Chester Harding. A fine portrait of the artist, painted by George W. Flagg in 1838, is now owned in Boston. Being a man of fine personal appearance and refined address, he married a Boston lady of exceptional beauty and wealth, and at once started upon an extended trip through Europe (1831–32), returning with a style materially changed, with more of the world in it, and less of true art. His popularity became greater ; but sober judgment pronounced his work deteriorated. His first work was characterized by warm tints and careful touches ; too careful, he thought afterward. They were sunny pictures, possessed of the pleasant grace of their author. In his second style his colors were leaden and cold, his work much more rapid and bolder. His early life gave a value to money, which produced a tendency to make a shrewd business-man of him ; a quality better for one's purse than his pictures, perhaps. For his skill at driving a bargain to his own advantage, Mr. Alexander won the title of "Art Jockey " among his friends. For instance, Charles Dickens was approaching America upon his first visit. The whole nation was on the *qui vive*. It was an event that was then looked forward to with as much expectancy as to-day would greet the Queen. The famous visitor was to land in Boston. Facilities were not so perfect then as now. It was impossible to say just when the steamer would arrive ; but, after insinuating himself into the good graces of that precarious pilot corps, Mr. Alexander kept himself so systematically on the alert, that he successfully boarded the steamer close behind the pilot, who, being an Irishman, left him the first American to greet the great arrival. He had hardly been introduced when he put the leading question, Would Mr. Dickens sit for his portrait? All he had expected was, at most, the refusal of the great man till the matter had been taken into consideration. To his surprise he received immediate consent, and the whole matter was at once arranged. Mr. Dickens, explaining the circumstance to friends afterward, said, "The impertinence of the thing was without limit; but the enterprise was most astonishing, and deserved any kind of a reward demanded." Of course the Alexander studio was the centre of popularity till the sittings and the picture were completed.

After his return from Europe he discovered that his tastes had been entirely changed. The atmosphere of New England was not more congenial than the farm had been in his boyhood. Florence offered much that could not be found in America; and, an acknowledged captive, he returned, where he now lives in peace and prosperity. At present it is his intention to take up a final residence in America during the fall of 1878.

THOMAS COLE.

It is an honor in art not to be over-valued, that, in the course of his eventful career, Thomas Cole became for a time a resident artist of Hartford. The Rev. L. L. Noble has given the world a volume concerning him that could not well be duplicated. A reference to it will be of much more value than any attempt to reduce its facts to a short article. He was born in Bolton-le-Moor, England, Feb. 1, 1801. His father failed in an extensive business. The boy, thrown from luxury to poverty, was obliged to enter into some employment. A clerkship in a law-office or in a manufacturer's counting-room was offered. The spirit that made the powerful devotee of art in later years persuaded him, against his own will even, to give them both up for a humble occupation, that in a very limited sense was creative. Later, when seventeen, he went to Liverpool to learn the trade of the wood-engraver. He was an inveterate reader, and had become so enthusiastic in a desire to see America, that he imparted his eagerness to his father, who, after failing in several efforts to re-establish himself, left for this country with all his family. Ill-luck did not desert him, however; and the boy was inured to the most tedious and unremitting labor, while the family moved from place to place in search of sufficient work to earn their bread.

Mr. Noble pays most complimentary attention to the boy's poetical ability, that strangely enough was inspired under such circumstances. A travelling portrait-painter gave him a book upon the first rules of art. It was a seed in good ground; and though he was obliged to make his own brushes, and borrow paint from a chair-maker, using a pine board for a palette, he was soon at work painting experimental portraits. A farmer of the village, who, inconsistently, had once been a pupil of Stuart's, was so much pleased with these endeavors, that he gave him a palette, colors, and brushes; and with this equipment, one dollar in his pocket, and a small change of clothing in a green sack over his shoulder, he started upon his first trip as an itinerant painter. His first order brought him a new saddle; his next, an old silver watch; then a chain and a watch-key (given for gold, which proved to be copper); another, a pair of shoes and a dollar. All these perquisites were ingulfed by the landlord's bill; and, as poor as ever, he started on. In the next place he just escaped arrest for a board-bill of thirty dollars through the kindness of four young men who stood bondsmen for him. Thus ill-luck followed him till he turned back in despair, and in one day walked sixty miles on his homeward journey. It was his last trial of the life of an itinerant. Struggle after struggle amounted to as little for him as for his father. Both seemed fated. His father, mercilessly driven to the very practical side of life, naturally opposed the boy's choice of art. His mother's sympathy had alone sustained him; and the time came at last when it was necessary to make a final determination, either to follow art to the end, or give it up forever. The young artist was walking in the field, after an excited talk with his father. He was tossing two pebbles in his hand. Suddenly he said to himself, "I will set one of these on a stick, and throw the other. If I knock it off the first time, I will go on in art; if I fail, I will give it up." A very great fate hung in a very small balance; but, guided by destiny, one pebble struck the other. He started in November for Philadelphia, taking with him his painting-materials, a very small supply of clothing, sixteen dollars in money, a mother's blessing, and a table-cover which she threw over his shoulders that lacked an overcoat. A most touching appeal to the sympathetic heart is the account which Mr. Noble gives of his early struggles in Philadelphia, where he passed his first winter in a musty upper room, living for the most part upon bread and water, warmed only by a broken cooking-stove, into the oven of which he was often obliged to thrust his legs to allay suffering, with the table-cover for his only blanket. One of the strangest facts connected with his life is that a series of comical paintings, the only specimens of the sort which he ever executed, emanated from this garret. In 1825 he moved to New York, where began almost instantaneously the fame that has made his name so great. He was, in the truest sense, a student of Nature. Every change in her swift vicissitudes, morning, noon, and night, were all familiarly known to him. While in London in 1829, he spent a fortnight with some relatives living a short distance from the city, in which place a revival was in progress. It was there that Mr. Cole's nature, always serious and upright, received the strong impress of religion which marked his life afterward. The exact time of Mr. Cole's life in Hartford it has been difficult to learn; probably in 1832–3. He came, in a sense, as *protegé* of Daniel Wadsworth, who was his firm friend through life. His studio was in the old Wadsworth mansion. He was very little known in the city, being of an exceedingly retiring disposition, and reluctant to be made the object of any notoriety whatever. Indeed, he is better known through the State to-day as the instructor of F. E. Church than even through his paintings. Several of his works are hung in the Athenæum Gallery, — "Mount Ætna," "A View in the White Mountains," "John the Baptist in the Wilderness," "A Cascade in the Catskills," "A View on Winnipiseogee Lake," and "Montevideo on Talcott Mountain." These pictures are so easy of access to the people of Connecticut, that no comment is necessary. The painting of Talcott Mountain has since been engraved. During his later years he painted with great rapidity, as the result of his lifelong study. He was the first thorough student of the Adirondacks, and a firm admirer of the beauties of the Catskills about his home, where he lived for many years, and where he died Feb. 11, 1848.

MOSELY ISAAC DANTFORTH.

An artist of merit earned by honest perseverance, M. I. Dantforth, was born in Hartford in 1801. When sixteen he began engraving under the direction of Asaph Willard in the Hartford Graphic Company. In three years he moved to New Haven, where he worked independently, and soon earned the reputation of being one of the best engravers of the country. Later he was among the principal movers in founding the American Bank-Note Company. In London, where he engraved Leslie's "Uncle Toby and the Widow," his work was pronounced "the very highest of engraving." This, however, is digressing. In 1825 he entered the National Academy at New York as a student, and, a year later, was elected an associate. In 1827 he went abroad, and undertook a course of art-study in the Royal Academy. In painting he pursued chiefly the branch of water-color, and early in his career made some copies of Titian and Paul Veronese that were very highly praised by the English press. In 1837 Mr. Dantforth returned to Connecticut, when much of his time was devoted to original water-color sketches that were very popular, and brought high prices. In 1858 he removed to New York, where he died four years later. Mr. Dantforth is spoken of, both in histories and by those who remember him well, as a man whose good qualities cannot be too highly estimated, an honor to art and society.

LOUIS FAIRCHILD.

The engraver Fairchild was born in Farmington, Conn., in the first year of the present century. He was also an artist of talent, though he left it unimproved. While studying engraving under Asaph Willard, he painted miniature portraits for the increase of his income. They were in exquisite color and delineation. One of Mrs. Lynch Botta would indicate that he made a great mistake in clinging to engraving. He was sensitive and over-critical about his work, but withal a true art-lover of the beautiful. At cost of many sacrifices, he purchased in Italy, and had brought to this country, a large cast of the Venus de' Medici. He kept it always closely veiled, and, when compelled to leave it at last, sooner than consign it to the hands of others, broke it in pieces with a hammer.

SAMUEL HOLT.

A portrait-painter, Samuel Holt, giving promise in his youth, was born in Meriden in 1801. He was unable to obtain instruction till he was thirty. Thereafter he painted miniature portraits very acceptably for four years, when failing eyesight drove him to the coarser work of car-decorating. He now resides in Hartford, and is the father of two sons, who, gathering his talent, have paid some attention to art; not, however, making it a professional life labor.

THOMAS H. PARKER.

A miniature-portrait painter, T. H. Parker, popular in Hartford in 1829 and thereabout, was born in Sag Harbor, L.I., in 1801. He studied under Matthew Rogers of New York, and settled at once in Hartford. He painted rapidly, and, being almost the only miniature-portrait painter in the State at the time, received very large patronage at good prices. One of his eccentricities was a pleasing habit of carrying a huge roll of bank-bills in his coat-pocket. Among his pupils in Hartford was C. W. El-dridge, still a resident of that city, who for many years was his partner, painting with him after the fashion of Waldo and Jewett. He was remarkably mild in temper. A youth in Hartford lost a ten-dollar wager that he could make him angry. His work all partook of this gentleness of spirit.

MILO HOTCHKISS,

A man of more ability than reputation, was born in Kensington, Conn., Oct. 10, 1802. He was a farmer's son, meeting with no advantages till about thirty, when he came to Hartford, and took a few lessons of Mr. Hewins. He was gaining considerable popularity in his work, when it became necessary for him to take his father's place upon the farm. Thereafter he did but little in art, and died Oct. 12, 1874.

THOMAS S. CUMMINGS.

By adoption at least, Gen. Thomas S. Cummings, born in 1804, may be claimed in the history of the State, having for many years resided in a beautiful home in Mansfield Centre. Mr. Dunlap devotes most honorable mention to him; and Professor Mapes shortly before his death wrote an exceedingly interesting biography, which, unfortunately, has not yet been published. Hence the liberty is taken to make several quotations from Professor Mapes's manuscript. Another claim which Connecticut may have upon Mr. Cummings is, that Augustus Earl, son of Ralph Earl, was the first to detect his ability, and to persuade his father to take him out of the counting-room where he had placed him, and send him instead to John R. Smith's drawing-school. During this instruction in drawing, the student developed such a talent that he was accepted as pupil by Henry Inman, then in the height of his popularity. He studied oil and water-color for three years with Mr. Inman; at the end of which time the artist paid him the extreme compliment of taking him into partnership as Inman & Cummings, eventually giving up to him the branch of miniature-portrait painting. Mr. Dunlap said of him, " He is the best-instructed painter of water-color portraits in the country." Mr. Cummings was one of the founders, and is one of three survivors among the founders, of the National Academy of Design, where for forty years he held the most responsible offices in the power of the institution to bestow.

Professor Mapes says, "Notwithstanding Mr. Cummings's proficiency in water-color, his friends all regretted the relinquishment, even in part, of oil-painting, as his proverbial accuracy and acquirements in the academic rules of art promised to place him at the head of any branch he might have chosen for his future practice." Professor Mapes vindicates the judgment of others in the statement, that, "since the time of the lamented Malbone, Cummings has been without a rival; and many of his works have furnished subjects to our best engravers, and ornamented the choicest annuals." "The Bride," "The Mother's Pearls," "The Exchange of Queens," "The Mysterious Lady," — engraved for the first number of "The Talisman," — are among the finest of these works. "The Bracelet," and "Ariadne," now in possession of Richard B. Hartshorne of New York, are also exquisite miniatures.

Of Mr. Cummings's connection with the National Academy of Design Professor Mapes says, "He was one of the most alive of its founders; its first treasurer; and, after thirty years of office, the Academy voted him a handsome service of plate." In 1831 he was elected by the Academy to a professorship, and proved a most valuable instructor. With a faculty unexcelled in matters of art, he combines an urbanity and generosity of

"THE BRACELET."—FROM THE PAINTING BY GEN. CUMMINGS.

deportment that render him a man invaluable to the art of the nation. This value Mr. Cummings has amply demonstrated as an active supporter of all of our philanthropic, learned, and social societies. The Lyceum of Natural History, the New-York Gallery of Fine Arts, the American and Mechanics' Institutes, the Century Club (of which he was one of the founders and first treasurer), and the Old Sketch Club, all owe much to his energy. He is also honorary member of many American and foreign academies of art. The University of New-York City also elected Mr. Cummings Professor of the Arts of Design, to fill the chair left vacant by the retirement of Professor Morse. At the same time Professor Cummings established his own and most eminently successful School of Design.

Mr. Cummings has also been an active man beyond the limits of the fine arts. He served in the uniform corps in every grade of the military service, and commanded the Second Regiment of Light Infantry, Washington Guards, for twelve years. Since his appointment to the rank of general, he has earned much power and obtained a high reputation as a military jurist, by virtue of his office receiving appeals, and confirming or reversing the decisions of courts-martial. It is noteworthy that these decisions have always been sustained when again appealed to a higher power. When but eighteen years old, Mr. Cummings married Miss Jane Cook; in which marriage (Gen. Cummings authorizes the statement) the population of the State was augmented by fourteen most excellent children.

An exceedingly interesting record of Mr. Cummings's services during his long connection with the National Academy is contained in his published work, "Annals of the National Academy of Design," which, with Mr. Dunlap's book, forms the only authentic history we have of the early days of art in America. Both books are scarce, having been published, unfortunately, by subscription. There are but a very few copies on sale; and, at the auction of Mr. Menzie's library a short time ago, a set of each, enriched with portraits, brought fifty-five dollars a volume.

A pleasant episode in the artist's life, given by permission, was the presentation by him to Queen Victoria of a copy of Mrs. Washington's portrait, and the reception of the following reply: —

SIR, — I have received and laid before the Queen your letter of the 9th of June, enclosing a portrait of Mrs. Washington, the wife of Gen. Washington, which you have painted from the original portrait by Gilbert Stuart, and which you have offered for the acceptance of her Majesty. The Queen commands me to acquaint you that she has very much admired the portrait, which, as a work of art, is of very high order, and will form a valuable addition to her Majesty's collection of historical portraits; together with the assurance of her Majesty's gratification at this proof of that kindly feeling toward her Majesty which has been so often expressed by citizens of the United States of America. I am also to transmit to you the accompanying gold medal, bearing the portrait of the Queen, which her Majesty requests you to accept as a mark of her regard.

I am, sir, your most obedient servant,

PALMERSTON.

To THOMAS S. CUMMINGS, Esq., New York.

During the erection of the present magnificent building of the National Academy of Design, for the sixth time he acted upon a building committee for that society, including in the course of such offices many important trusts.   In one single dealing he made for the National Academy the sum of sixty-one thousand dollars, which formed the nucleus for its present wealth and luxurious independence.   It should justly be added, however, that to the form of the present Academy Building Gen. Cummings was opposed, thinking it much wiser to have the lower story of stores that should render an income toward the support of the galleries, but was over-ruled by the rest.   When the building was finished, having completed his fortieth year of service, he resigned his treasurership, and retired to his present lovely home in Mansfield Centre, to rest in the valley of the Fenton under his own vine and maple, — a rare selection, a fortunate choice for the calm and quiet of the great artist reformer, and more fortunate for the people of Connecticut with whom he lives.

GEN. CUMMINGS'S HOUSE, CONNECTICUT.

Like all his other works of art, Gen. Cummings's house in Mansfield Centre is a gem.   It stands on the site of the old block-house fort erected for defence against the Indians, and some of the original white-oak beams are used in the present structure.

The soldier-artist has lived a most valuable life, the more so in that he has lived it in advance of his associates, and, by earnestness, nobility, and generosity, urged them to higher walks.   May he yet live to see the full results of his life's labor, when the standard he has urged shall have been gained, when Athena shall sit upon the throne with the Goddess of Liberty, and hand in hand, as one royal sovereign, Freedom and Beauty, inseparable forevermore, shall lead the world onward and upward!

JAMES HAMILTON SHÉGOGUE.

April 7, 1872, there died in Warrenville, Conn., where he had resided for ten years, the well-known and talented artist James H. Shégogue. His profession was portraiture, though many ideal and some historical pieces were produced on his easel. He was French by descent, born in Charleston, S.C., Feb. 22, 1806. He began his professional work in New York, 1836; and remained there, except during several trips to Europe, till his removal to Warrenville in 1862. The work which first brought him into notice was "An Old Straw Hat," with a boy under it, across whose face the sun shone in patches corresponding with rents in the hat. It was exhibited in the American Academy of Art, and praised by its president, Col. Trumbull. While copying Guido's "Aurora" in the Borghese Palace at Rome for Mr. Penniman of New York, the Princess Borghese pronounced his work the best copy she had ever seen. He was a member of the Old Sketch Club and of the Century Club, and in 1843 was elected an academician in the National Academy, of which in 1849 he became corresponding secretary. His income from his work was large; but, tiring of the noise of New York, he came for quiet to the banks of the Mount-Hope River, where he pursued his work with unremitted enthusiasm until within a few weeks of his death. Some of his last works are in possession of S. R. Arnold, Esq., of Willimantic. Portraits of two of Gen. Cummings's daughters are among his best work; also an excellent group, the children of Secretary Fish. "The Chinaman from Birth to Grave," and "The Heathen Chinee," two series in possession of Mr. Gillman of New York, are powerful and poetic in treatment and æsthetic effect. He was a man of unusual education, a proficient linguist, and scientific explorer. A large picture, "Christ Betrayed," is owned by the Baptist Society of Warrenville, and hangs in the church. Another large picture executed at Warrenville, "Landing of Chinese Women," is owned in Willimantic by Mr. Royce. As a man and artist Mr. Shégogue exerted an influence, doing honor to both, which cannot soon be forgotten.

PHILIP HEWINS.

The portrait-painter Hewins, who figured conspicuously in the art of Connecticut from 1834 to 1850, was born at Blue Hill, Me., in July, 1806. When two years of age he was taken by his parents to Sharon, Mass., about eighteen miles from Boston. He displayed the early propensities of the artist, but in youth entered into the dry-goods business in Boston and elsewhere, in which he made a remarkably successful beginning.

While in Albany, having his portrait painted by one Reuben Roulery, he rediscovered his artistic ability, and studied under him a year, thereafter devoting himself to self-instruction and the practice of art. He came to Hartford in 1834, having already established for himself a name of importance in art. His first portrait in that city was of the Right Rev. T. H. Brownell, Bishop of Connecticut; followed soon by one of the Rev. Dr. Hawes, Mrs. Sigourney, Major George Goodwin, Hon. J. M. Niles, and others, fully confirming his previous reputation, and giving him a popularity that held him in Hartford till his death, which occurred suddenly, May 14, 1850. For some time he was the first portrait-painter in Hartford, and gave lessons to many who have since gained high positions in art. But his attention was somewhat devoted to invention, and the mining projects of California, toward the latter part of his life, when his work became unequal and somewhat deteriorated. Beside his work in portraiture, he painted five large scriptural pieces on seven-feet-by-nine canvases, which were first exhibited in the lecture-room of the Centre Church, Hartford, and very highly commended. He possessed a faculty of rapid execution, and gave evidence of brilliant genius. His touch was bold and free. His pictures indicate an excellent taste and feeling for color, and were often pronounced fine likenesses.

SOLOMON FANNING.

Solomon Fanning, born in Preston, Conn., 1807, went to New York in 1833, and studied portrait-painting. In 1840 he settled in Norwich, where, for four years, he practised his profession with considerable success. His portraits are said to have been good likenesses. In 1850 lack of work induced him to forsake portraiture for ornamental work upon cars. Mr. Fanning still resides in Norwich.

ELLSWORTH.

An artist named Ellsworth, born in Windsor early in 1807, son of one of the officers in charge of the State House for many years, first displayed a taste for art in making several copies of Gilbert Stuart's full-length of Gen. Washington. The copies are neither extraordinarily good nor very bad: one hanging in the Wadsworth Gallery shows chiefly a lack of experience and information. He was very eccentric, kept himself away from society, and read Shakspeare incessantly. At last too much Shakspeare made him mad. He married unhappily, which had a tendency in the same direction, and left without warning for the West. He appeared

H. C. Shumway

in St. Louis, and painted "A Wounded Grecian Racer," which created much excitement. It was remarked by artists as "a wild conception, good in color, fine drawing, and altogether praiseworthy." The artist next appeared in Connecticut, a weather-beaten wanderer, followed by an old dog, which, he said, was his only friend on earth. He stopped at a farm-house near Hartford, and offered to paint the family in exchange for food and old clothes. The pictures, though painted under such fearful circumstances, show withal a lingering shadow of the hand that wrought the "Grecian Racer." The strange artist died in an almshouse in Pittsburgh in 1874.

HENRY C. SHUMWAY.

On the 4th of July, 1807, Henry C. Shumway, the soldier-artist, was born in Middletown, Conn. His patriotic birthday indexed the military career in which he has gained renown; his school-days, the artist. On a long, high board fence skirting the road opposite the school, the boy, destined to be one of the foremost miniature-portrait painters of America, was wont to relieve the pressure of destiny, and amuse his schoolfellows, with life-size caricatures of friends and foes, often bearing excellent likenesses. When his school-days were over, his father took him into his office. This course did not satisfy either the fancy or ambition; and so much of his time was expended upon pencil-sketches (as so much of his time in school had been devoted to chalk-drawings), that his father found a difficult task before him; and the boy waited only for the freedom of one and twenty years to place himself as a student in the National Academy at New York. For two years he attended the antique and life schools; then established himself as an artist, strictly a painter of miniature portraits on ivory. He has worked only in oil as a temporary relaxation or experimentally, and has remained in New York with but transient exceptions. At one time he painted for several months in Washington upon the heads of celebrated national officers, many times for the summer in Middletown, and occasionally in Hartford. During his visits in the latter city his headquarters were with Daniel Wadsworth, and his studio at one time in the daguerrotype-gallery of J. W. Stancliff.

Mr. Shumway began painting in 1829 for ten dollars a miniature portrait. His popular success cannot be better estimated than in the fact, that, in the prosperous days of miniature-painting in America, he reached a dignity of reputation that gave him three hundred dollars for a portrait upon five-inch ivory. His principal work in Washington was a fine portrait of Henry Clay. In Hartford he painted Judge Storrs, Gov. Trumbull's family, Col. Wadsworth, and others. In 1832 he was made an academician.

About 1860 photographs had taken such a popular position in the country, that he was obliged to look beyond his orders for miniature portraits on ivory for constant occupation. The same material, and much the same process, which is used in miniatures, is introduced in coloring photographs; and this branch of the art Mr. Shumway undertook for the sake of the occupation. This labor he still pursues in the studio he has occupied for many years on Broadway. He is a man of decided culture and intelligence, of invariable politeness, and an untiring energy within and without the confines of art. He was prominent in forming and sustaining the Seventh New-York Regiment, which he afterwards commanded with distinction. For thirty-five years he has belonged to the New-York State militia; and, after serving as captain for twenty-eight years, is now honorably brevetted.

Both in his military and civil character, Mr. Shumway has been the recipient of many laudations. An eminent artist, a respected critic, and a soldier of high rank, who has long and intimately known Mr. Shumway, writes of him: "He is a man in every way worthy of the highest commendation. I never heard an ill word of him from any one. A quiet, retiring, and upright man, — perhaps too retiring to be as well known as he should be; yet he is very well known, and everywhere highly thought of."

In 1844 the artist received the gold palette for the best miniature portrait in the art-exhibition of the State Fair. In 1838 he painted a large miniature head of Napoleon III. from life, which is now in possession of the family of the late Rev. Mr. Stewart, for a long time of the United-States navy.

JOSEPH IVES PEASE.

One of the remarkable men of Connecticut in many ways is J. I. Pease, engraver, poet, inventor, crayon-artist, and water-colorist; for several years past an extensive farmer as well, on "Brook-Trout Farm," upon Twin Lakes, Salisbury, Conn. He was born in Norfolk, Litchfield County, Conn., Aug. 9, 1809; and, after going through all the activities of a boy whose eyes and ears are wide open to what is possible in the world, juvenile experiments and inventions of all sorts, he was finally, at the age of fourteen, placed in a dry-goods store of Hartford, to the end that he might expend his energy on the practical side of life. It was too practical for him, or, more properly, not practical enough; and he hailed the day when he was sent home in disgrace. He was fortunately consulted as to his next apprenticeship, and chose a position under Oliver Pelton of Hartford to learn the art of engraving. This has been his life-work; and, as not within the precincts of the present subject, a large part of his interesting history must be dropped until a later volume. Crayon-drawing he studied for two winters in the National Academy at New York. His chief work, as crayon artist and painter, was performed in Philadelphia,

JOSEPH IVES PEASE.

where he settled in 1835, making many crayon heads at good prices, and giving lessons to a number of pupils. His son, a rising water-color artist, is mentioned later. He is still actively engaged in the pursuits of his life.

SETH W. CHENEY.

That man is rarely found of whom one may speak wisely, and not too well. Such a man, however, was Seth W. Cheney, born in South Manchester in 1810, a member of the family so widely associated with the silk-manufactories of Connecticut. As a student in art, and a man in the world, he was every thing that student and man could be. The influence of his brother, John Cheney the engraver, was obvious in guiding well at the outset the first thoughts of art, thus rendering more easily attainable the future excellence. From the study of engraving, natural inclination made an easy step into the art of crayon-drawing. In this branch Mr. Cheney secured the great success of his life, that has placed his name nobly and indelibly in the history of American art. To the casual observer it sometimes appears, that because this is the first thing taught the student in painting, and the beginning of all the arts of design, — the simplest form of the art, in fact, — it is also the lowest. A little thought will disclose a vital error. Drawing is essential to every artist; but, over this, color is a very serviceable cloak, that often covers a multitude of sins. They are to be found even among the masters, whose seductive coloring enhances a result so erroneous in drawing, that, if the outline were to be left naked, a child could better it. Drawing is made the figure which color clothes, and clothes gracefully; but surely, if it were necessary to institute a comparison between the two, the greater art would be to make the perfect figure,

"MEMORY." — FROM A CRAYON-DRAWING MADE BY SETH CHENEY FOR MRS. A. L. BOTTA.

in complete grace and loveliness, with light and shadow, life and character, in simple black and white. This distinction Mr. Cheney felt, and often expressed with great force. It was so apparent to him, that once, when induced to attempt work in oil (in which good critics assured him he met with admirable success), he immediately laid down his palette again in much the same spirit that David discarded the armor of Saul, satisfied that color was an incumbrance for him to avoid. He was the first to give the art of crayon-drawing independent prominence in the United States. It was looked upon much as water-color painting has been regarded until within a few years. It required a bold and efficient man to place himself

S. B. Chiney.

as its advocate, with nothing to sustain him but his ability in that one branch; but he championed the art so effectively, that while in Paris, the home of crayon-artists, he won for himself public acknowledgment as "the greatest American artist in crayon-drawing."

In personal appearance Mr. Cheney was tall and thin, with light hair, gray eyes, a high forehead, and remarkably fine-shaped head. At times through his life he was afflicted with a severe pain in his head, which materially interrupted his work. He was extremely social within a limited circle of friends, but, beyond it, reserved and retiring. A natural reluctance to making new friends asserted itself powerfully in his work, where he found it so difficult that he sometimes refused to execute a portrait when he discovered what he termed a "moral antagonism" between himself and his sitter, — a sacrifice rarely made to art.

During his study of art Mr. Cheney made four trips to Europe, spending most of his time in Paris and Rome. In Rome he placed himself under the instruction of Ferrero, who, at parting, pronounced his eye for color equal to his drawing. Mr. Cheney was, however, over-ready to admit that even his drawing was very imperfect; and only the great demand made upon him, through the wide popular reputation he had gained, prevented him from withdrawing from public view altogether, killed by his own criticism. The case of the oil-portraits of Mr. E. W. Bull the druggist, and wife, executed on his return from Rome, was but an exaggerated example of his opinion of all of his work. The pictures present every indication of refinement, good taste, and ability, — genius, in fact; but the artist failed to see his own power, and for a long time refused to touch the brush again for any work whatever. Toward the close of his life, however, he did some very fine ideal work in oil. His greatest power was in obtaining a thoroughly expressive likeness, indicative of individuality in wonderful detail. He worked rapidly, sometimes completing a bust portrait in six hours. Naturally, his critical mind prevented much of his ideal work from ever coming into public view; and from his evident masterpiece, the "Head of a Roman Girl," it may only be surmised how much valuable work has been lost to the world in the artist's repeated destruction of his own productions.

He was a genius in the full sense of that expressive word, unequalled in the delicate delineation of the female head, a keen lover of all beauty, particularly susceptible to any discord, fastidious, sympathetic, and withal possessing a strong personality. His tastes in art were too refined, his standard too high, to allow the possibility of satisfaction. To the persevering encouragement of his wife, Mrs. Ednah D. Cheney, must be credited much of his later work, which would otherwise have probably been left undone, or destroyed even before it was finished.

His death, which occurred in his native village in 1856, was the result of a lingering, calm decline, and was fitly supplemented by a moonlight burial.

C. W. ELDRIDGE.

A member of the old miniature-portrait firm of Parker & Eldridge, C. W. Eldridge, born in New London, Conn., in November, 1811, at present resides in Hartford. He studied for a year under T. H. Parker in Hartford; then entered into partnership with him, which continued for nine years, when Mr. Parker was disabled by disease. Shortly after the partnership was formed they went to New York, remaining a little over a year; then upon an extended trip through the South. For three years after Mr. Parker's withdrawal, Mr. Eldridge continued miniature-portrait painting in the South; but photographs reducing the orders, and trouble with his eyes, induced him to abandon art.

JOHN MITCHELL.

An intimate friend of the artist John Mitchell asserts that he was born in Hartford, 1811. He spent his life in Hartford, with the exception of the years 1857–8, when he lived in New London. He was handsome, good-natured, and tragic in manner. He often played Richard III. in Wyat's company, at the City-Hotel Hall; and painted with a bold, free hand that invariably made an attractive portrait, and gave him as extensive a local popularity as he could have desired. Throughout his life, however, he was fiercely addicted to liquor, and, in 1866, died an unfortunate death in the New-York Hospital as the result.

WILLIAM PAGE.

It cannot well be considered borrowing another's laurels, though William Page was born in Albany, N.Y., 1811, to note that in 1848 he was painting in Middletown, Conn. This greatest explorer in art, the ardent enthusiast, never lost an opportunity, throughout his eventful activity, to impart to any willing listener his various theories, and to explain the peculiarities of the system he was investigating in the picture he was painting at the time. Being well informed himself, he could not fail of producing impressions strongly savored with valuable hints, regardless of the importance of his immediate subject. It is a most interesting occupation to trace the train set on fire by an intelligent enthusiast, in whatever department. The results of Mr. Page's visit in Middletown may be easily recognized long afterward.

JOSEPH ROPES.

A popular crayon-artist and drawing-teacher since, the landscape-painter Joseph Ropes resided in Hartford from 1851 to 1865, when he sailed for Europe, where he remained in Italy for eleven years, returning to America to establish himself in Philadelphia, where he still resides. Among other valuable influences he has exerted for art is one in the shape of a volume on "Linear Perspective," widely used over the State and elsewhere. Several prominent artists of to-day were under his direction when in Hartford; and many friends remember him with great admiration, both as a careful, tasteful, successful artist, and admirable gentleman. He was born in Salem, Mass., 1812. Always intent upon art, unavoidable circumstances prevented his undertaking the study till in his thirty-fifth year. Then he studied with John R. Smith in New York, and also in the National Academy.

HENRY BRYANT.

A most estimable man, combining the graces of humanity and the love of art, Henry Bryant, a native of East Hartford, was born in 1812. His boyhood was in neither extreme of opulence or poverty. A good common-school education laid the foundation for the life of valuable thought and investigation that has followed it. A native tendency toward art was early manifest in the passion for picture-making, with any material that offered the greatest facilities at the time; and successful caricatures often brought the schoolboy into the depths of bitterness. Another bent was also developed with even more force than art in a strongly scientific turn of mind. Both fortunately and unfortunately, a double die was cast. By coincidence one course of life was pointed out to him, by necessity another. He was assisting in hoeing potatoes one summer afternoon, when a laborer working near him stopped, leaned upon his hoe, and said, "Do you know, boy, they say this world is round." It was a fact not at all new, or newly put; but the moment was the one chosen by Destiny. A door was suddenly opened in the commonplace utterance, by which he entered into the vast researches of astronomy. This study has been his life's labor, at times even greatly at the expense of his art. His astronomical inventions are both numerous and valuable.

The pathway into art was opened to him when, but fifteen years old, he was placed as apprentice under Mr. E. Huntington to learn the trade of the engraver. This occupation he pursued for five years, during the latter part of which time he painted several portraits of acquaintances with such success, that at twenty he gave up engraving, and secured instruction in art from John Coles.   After studying a year, having mastered the rudiments and developed a decided taste, he became, as was the popular custom of the day, an itinerant portrait-painter.   After two years of this, he opened a studio in the city of New York.   He was an artist of personal popularity there, as many letters received from his friends of that period unhesitatingly assert.   In 1837 he was made an associate of the National Academy of Design, being proposed by Professor Morse.   Three years afterward he married, and returned to his father's home, where, and in Hartford, he practised portrait-painting for four years.   He was, with James Willard, in 1844, the first to take up the daguerrotype; and spent the next two years in Virginia, making it a successful experiment.   In

HENRY BRYANT.

1850 he began a more careful study of landscape-painting, which he has since pursued in an equal degree with portrait-painting, in the same studio (the one which he now occupies), for a quarter of a century.

In theology, as well as art and science, Mr. Bryant's life has been one of peculiar thought and investigation.   From holding precisely opposite ideas, he has by slow degrees been led to adopt the full theory of the Spiritualists.   Resulting from this is a large study, yet unfinished, "The Spirit's Birth," a thoroughly original and strongly imaginative conception, arranged with excellent effect of light and shade.   He has at present upon his easel a view of Lake George, of merit both in drawing and coloring. Many landscapes and ideal pieces of Mr. Bryant's painting are owned in Hartford.   Few men have succeeded in a long life in building and sustaining such a kindly reputation as graces Mr. Bryant. A New-York artist of celebrity writes of him, "As a man and a friend I never met his equal." Another: "I once went on a sketching trip with him up your beautiful Connecticut Valley, and found him, there as everywhere else, generous, enthusiastic, and industrious."

CHARLES LORING ELLIOTT.

In 1865, for the fourth time, Charles L. Elliott visited Hartford, set up his easel, and advertised for orders. Among the works which he executed were full-length portraits of Samuel Colt's family. There are some who consider him the greatest portrait-painter of America. It is more probable that he *might* have been. In character, modelling, and drawing he had great merit. He never fully succeeded in delineating a female face; but his forte, in which certainly few ever excelled him, lay in depicting the bronzed lines of age, the furrows and wrinkles of character, and in translating them correctly. His flesh-tints were admirable; and gray hair, under his touch, became literally "a crown of glory." Many consider Mr. Elliott's best portraits two that he painted for his brother-artist F. E. Church, — one of the artist himself; the other of his father, the late Joseph Church of Hartford, — both in possession of Mrs. Joseph Church. Mr. Elliott was born in Scipio, N.Y., 1812. His life was one continuous struggle against obstacles, and at last the yielding of one overcome. He was a man proverbially quick in wit. James Beard, at a dinner, responding to the toast "High Art," said that Elliott had lately told him he had made up his mind that high art in America was the shape of the canvas and the depth of the frame. Elliott was engaged to paint the portrait of Daniel Webster, when the statesman's last sickness prevented.

HENRY C. FLAGG.

The name of Flagg is most intimately associated with art in Connecticut. Already five children and children's children of the late Mayor Flagg of New Haven have appeared before the easel. The blood of their uncle Washington Allston, brother-in-law of Mayor Flagg, is strongly asserted in his nephews. The oldest son, Henry C. Flagg, was born in New Haven in 1812. When a child, returning from South Carolina, he, with the rest of the passengers, was made a prisoner by an English frigate. This early tragedy gave a spice to life upon the sea that never wore off. In school he was the popular caricaturist, and celebrated among the juveniles for his successful likenesses on blackboards, doors, and old

plank fences. When sixteen, the charms of the sea drew him into the
navy. In 1832 he returned to New Haven, and began painting. His
passion was still for marine-views, though he also developed much skill in
animal-drawing. But the navy offered more than art, and he went back
to sea ; though he compromised by taking his easel with him, and painting
whenever time and tide allowed. From the deck of a man-of-war he
painted a marine-view, which he exhibited in Brazil, and was made a member of the Imperial Academy. He died at Jamestown during the Rebellion, just after receiving command of a Northern ship. It would evidently
be unjust to judge of his ability by his work, though a favorable criticism
might be offered.

CHAUNCEY B. IVES.

The sculptor C. B. Ives was born in Hamden, Conn., in 1812. He was
a farmer's son, and apparently destined to become himself a farmer. But
the yoke was unbearable ; and when sixteen he apprenticed himself to E.
R. Northrup, wood-carver, and, later, studied for a short time with Hezekiah Augur. After rapidly consuming all that he found to be learned in
New Haven, he went to Boston. His stand in art had been very timid.
He did not know himself. He locked himself in his room in Boston, and
worked. He did his utmost to discover how much that was. The result
was a fine marble bust, which shortly afterward won for him a gold medal.
Orders began to accumulate ; and he soon formed the plan of removing to
Florence, Italy, for better facilities. He spent six years there ; then went
to Rome, where he has now resided for twenty-five years, with the exception of transient visits in America. This is partially for his art, and also
for his health ; four brothers and sisters having died of consumption.
When taking some casts in Meriden, Conn., in 1841, a physician whom he
consulted warned him that he was rapidly declining with the same disease.
His characteristic comment to a friend was, " I shall not consult that man
again."

In 1855 Mr. Ives opened a studio in New York, intending to remain
two years. This studio, a marvel of beauty, is justly spoken of at length
by Mr. Tuckerman. It was adorned with much of the artist's original
work that had already attained great excellence. Orders appeared so
rapidly, that in two months he returned to Rome. Mr. Ives was given
the State order for the statues of Gov. Trumbull and Roger Sherman for
the Washington Monument. The fine piece of bronze, Bishop Brownell,
on the Trinity-College grounds in Hartford, is also his. His bust of the
great architect Towne is one of the finest pieces of marble in the Yale
Art Collection. His work is invariably pleasing, and well executed. His

ideal subjects are from the commonplaces of life, magically treated in an easy and refined manner. He is a careful student and industrious artist. His success has been great. In 1862 he married, and now has a family of five children.

WILLIAM JAMES LINTON.

The wood-engraver, designer, and water-color artist, W. J. Linton, of extended repute both in Europe and America, has resided in New Haven for the past eight years. He was born in London, 1812; and, though his life has been devoted to designing and engraving, he has also achieved prominent success in water-color painting. He is a member of the Society of Painters in Water-Colors. A complete history of his remarkable life is contained in Routledge's "Men of the Time."

LUTHER TERRY.

In the town of Enfield, Conn., Luther Terry was born in 1813. He passed his boyhood there, but when seventeen years old came to Hart-

LUTHER TERRY.

ford, and was apprenticed to a bookbinder. He learned the trade, but found it wholly unsatisfactory, and gradually turned his attention toward portraiture, for which he had always realized a fond ambition. He began study under Philip Hewins; but in 1838, before his position in art could be established, he went to Italy, where he has since remained, with the exception of occasional visits to America. His first year he passed in Florence, studying in the Imperial and Royal Academy, and copying in the galleries; then went to Rome, which has since been his home. In Rome he began studying and drawing from the antique and life, from the frescos by Raffaelle, under a master, spending the summer in Venice. Mr. Terry has built up a high reputation, and met with most flattering success. He has produced many ideal pieces upon large canvases, chiefly scriptural subjects, that are owned in various parts of America. One of these, possessing much merit, though among his early works, hangs in the Wadsworth Athenæum Gallery. The coloring is especially interesting, as well as the modelling. His style has developed into a decided Tintoretto, with a strong feeling for bright color. He has been among the most popular of American artists in Italy, possessing, in portraiture especially, peculiar power. He is an excellent colorist, and extremely careful and conscientious in execution. His refined taste, and delicate appreciation of character and female grace, will long preserve his name as an important factor in the art of America. He is a man of wide information, and a keen sense of justice. His ideal pieces are comparatively few, but exceptionally fine. His first exhibition at the Academy in 1854 was an ideal female head, that justly won almost unlimited praise.

He has upon his easel, nearly completed at the present time, a work of three years, pronounced one of his best paintings. It is "Solomon's Dream." The central figure lies asleep. In the background are allegorical figures of Wisdom, Riches, Honor, Fame, Beauty, each followed by a child bearing an appropriate token. These figures are enveloped in a bright light, contrasting with the light of a lamp burning at the head of the sleeping figure. It possesses marked merit in design, as well as execution.

S. S. LYMAN.

Sylvester S. Lyman, at present and for many years a portrait-painter in Hartford, born in Easthampton, Mass., Sept. 24, 1813, began the study of portraiture under Mr. Hewins in Hartford in 1839, continuing it later under Edwin White. Within a few years he has devoted more attention to landscape-painting; and, finding sufficient patronage in Hartford, has done but little elsewhere.

J. W. STANCLIFF.

For many years the marine-painter J. W. Stancliff has occupied a studio in Hartford. He was born in Chatham, Conn., on the east bank of the river, in 1814. From childhood his propensities were all with the sea;

and, when the love of art obtained an influential hold upon his life, naturally the first and strongest impressions were of the sea. His knowledge of waves and shipping is extraordinary. Opportunities for an art-education were limited; but nature and love have done much for him. His first steps in color were taken when sixteen, through the proverbial medium of the carriage-shop; after which he also studied copperplate engraving. He taught the first drawing-class established in America, in connection with regular public-school exercises, earnestly supported by the Rev. Thomas H. Gallaudet. He studied oil-painting under A. H. Emmons and J. B. Flagg, and water-color under Benjamin H. Coe. During a connection of fifteen years with telegraphy, he made drawings of the "House" and "Combination" instruments on exhibition in Hartford, which won for him the gold medal. He has painted extensively on the Atlantic coast; and his views are of great variety, possessing much merit as honest representations, and specimens of fidelity to the subject, more acceptable than frequent in marine-work. He is President of the Connecticut School of Design, and an enthusiastic supporter of art.

GEORGE H. CUSHMAN.

It has been a policy strictly observed in these sketches, for several reasons thought desirable, to avoid inserting *verbatim* any correspondence, either from the artist in question or from his friends. Just once this rule will be overstepped. Concerning the miniature-portrait painter George H. Cushman, whose life, celebrated as it was, was much more a private than a public life, two characteristic letters have been received from persons most intimately acquainted with the true nature of the artist, and of all writers best fitted to portray it. Many other sketches would have been much improved by this same adoption, had not certain general objections prevented.

Mr. Cushman was born June 5, 1814, in Windham, Conn. He was in many respects a superior artist, with a peculiar faculty for drawing rapidly, effectively, and correctly. Among many excellent miniature paintings which he left in Hartford is one of Daniel Wadsworth. His coloring was characteristically soft and pleasing. He did not adopt the art in which he displayed such talent till comparatively late in life, having first mastered the art of engraving under Asaph Willard in Hartford. He was a fine water-colorist in every department, and some of his last and best work was done in Newington. Grace Greenwood writes: "I am happy to learn that you are writing a sketch of our noble friend George Cushman. I felt that not enough was said at the time of his death,—a

death which seemed to his friends as untimely as it was sad ; which took
from us a warm, true, loyal heart, companionship the most genial, friendship the most generous yet just, the most ardent yet reliable, and from
the life of art a hand of cunning, a fancy of rare refinement, an eye and
thirst for beauty, perceptions the most quick and accurate, a fine intuition
of color, an instinct of grace, a soul for all the spiritual meanings and har-
monies of art.   His miniature works were always remarkable for purity
and simplicity of character as well as tone.   The best and sweetest and
truest traits of his sitters he could call forth and fix in those fairy portraits.
The most minute of his male heads were remarkable for an air of earnest
manhood.   The most exquisite of his female heads were distinguished by

GEORGE H. CUSHMAN.

a certain breadth and depth of womanliness, giving them a dignity which
mere grand proportions cannot give.   Cushman seemed to me to work in
the essence of color, so wondrously soft yet clear were his tints, so
dreamy, so aerially delicate, were his lights and shades.   To our friend,
as a man, could truly have been applied that much-abused term 'chival-
rous.'   He was ever ready to champion the weak and the wronged ; and
his indignation against injustice, and his scorn of meanness, were something worth seeing.   He was intense in his likes and dislikes ; but, while
he never 'went back' on a friend, he never revenged himself on an enemy.
Life was not a holiday to him, but it was not a wearisome task-day.   He
found much beauty in nature, much good in humanity.   He never lost
his faith in his fellow, or his faith in his Father."

Mrs. Botta writes : "My acquaintance with Mr. Cushman dates back to the period of early youth, and an unbroken friendship of so many years' standing gave me every opportunity of knowing and appreciating the many noble qualities he possessed. His character was a rare combination of masculine strength and feminine purity and delicacy. He had a high sense of honor, which led him to detest every thing that was base and unworthy, and a love for the good and the beautiful that made him venerate and admire whatever appealed to that sense, whether he found it in art, in nature, or in his fellow-beings. Sincerity was another marked trait, which rendered him incapable of untruthfulness or dissimulation ; and his naturalness and simplicity of character made him impatient of vanity and affectation, in whatever form or in whatever persons they manifested themselves. His modesty was so extreme, that it became a defect ; for, with a higher and more just estimation of himself, he would have accomplished more, and impressed others with a more true idea of his merits. His early tastes were for a military education at West Point, and an army life ; but he was prevented from following his inclinations, and he remained in civil life, where he was to some extent misplaced. The powerful frame, exuberant vitality, and commanding presence, that made the ideal of a military hero, seemed not to have found their highest or rather their widest sphere in the artist's studio.

"The personal appearance of Mr. Cushman may be best described by the word *distinguished.* In the street, in the crowded assembly, wherever he went, people asked, 'Who is he?' and the impression produced by his strikingly fine head and well-proportioned figure was deepened by the entire unconsciousness of his manner.

"Outside of the limit of private life Mr. Cushman was chiefly known as an artist, and under different circumstances he would have taken the highest rank as a miniature painter. But, as I have said, he was inclined to under-estimate his own genius ; he lacked the stimulus of pecuniary necessity ; and for many years he suffered from an intensely painful malady which to some extent paralyzed alike his ambition and his physical energy. The pictures he painted were done mostly for his friends, and not professionally. They are of unequal merit ; but of the best of them it is not too much to say, that they compare favorably with those of Malbone, if they do not equal them ; and, if he had devoted himself to the art, he would have achieved a renown as high."

More than this could not be added. Mr. Cushman died in Jersey City, Aug. 3, 1876, at a water-cure establishment.

DENISON KIMBERLY.

The engraver Denison Kimberly, born in Guilford, 1814, of parents too poor to offer him any facilities, early determined upon a life of art. He said of himself that he earned just enough at clam-digging to learn how to make a clam in crayon, when he discovered that he could not support himself, and study too ; and was obliged to accept the next best thing, and be an engraver. He was a fellow-pupil with George H. Cushman under Asaph Willard, who, in the course of his life, has instructed so many prominent engravers. Mr. Kimberly took a high position among them ; but in 1858 the passion to paint overcame the pride in his present success, and he went to Boston to study oil. For four years after his return he painted in Hartford and Manchester. A fine specimen of his work is a portrait of Seth Cheney, strong in outline, but remarkably soft in feature ; a good likeness, and the work of a bold, free hand.

GEORGE A. GILBERT.

George A. Gilbert, an Englishman of extensive and well-earned reputation, came to Hartford in 1874. William Howitt, the English historian, says of him, " He was a man of superior education, much reading, an active and accomplished mind, a good artist, and devoted to his work with an indefatigable zeal." He was born in Chichester, Eng., in 1815 ; and died in Hartford Dec. 23, 1877. During his residence in Hartford he was a successful teacher, and delivered several entertaining lectures on art in Springfield. His qualifications in art were very versatile. Naturally talented, he had attained an unusual degree of proficiency in many branches. His characteristic success was in drawing forest-trees, either in oil, water-color, pencil, crayon, pen, or chalk.

ALFRED HART.

In 1838 Alfred Hart began the study of art in Norwich, Conn., where he was born March 28, 1816. He went to New York to continue his study, established himself as an artist in Norwich, and in 1848 moved to Hartford, where he prepared and exhibited a huge panorama of " Pilgrim's Progress." His work was largely bought by Albert Day. It was good in many respects ; but Mr. Hart has never devoted the undivided attention to art that makes the proficient. He has invented several useful machines ; and for nearly twenty-five years he has lived in the West, sketching, painting, and introducing his inventions.

DANIEL HUNTINGTON.

The President of the National Academy, Daniel Huntington, the famous portrait-painter, though born in the "Old Dutch City" (in 1816), is, after all, by virtue of a long line of ancestors and his own school-days and early art-days, an artist of Connecticut: yet so many able pens have lauded his virtues, and wisely extolled his wonderful talents, that it would be useless to make another attempt in these pages. In Yale the first inclination toward art appeared in successful caricatures. These were strengthened by repeated visits to Col. Trumbull's studio, and in 1835 he began the direct study of art under Professor Morse. Four years later

DANIEL HUNTINGTON.

he went abroad, studying in Florence and Rome, and, after returning, completed his study under William Page. In 1850 he returned for a short time to New Haven to paint the portraits of Professors Silliman and Dana on an order from William P. Wright, who proposed a gallery of the leading living artists, scientists, literati, and merchants. To Thomas Hicks was given the order for the writers, to Rossiter the merchants, to Baker the artists, and to Mr. Huntington the order for the scientific men. Eight years previously he had painted for some time in Thompsonville on a large order from Mr. Thompson. Mr. Huntington has also been an elegant and entertaining writer; which occupation, however, a slight trouble with his eyes has caused him to abandon.

WILLIAM KÖHNER.

A German portrait-painter, William Köhner, born in Berlin 1816, settled in Hartford in 1853, remaining there in active occupation till 1866, when he removed to Warehousepoint, Conn., where he died ten years later. He painted a smooth, flat picture; but obtained a likeness at a low price, and had an abundance of orders. One of the best pictures he painted was of Gov. Seymour.

A. H. EMMONS.

For the past thirty years A. H. Emmons has painted portraits in Norwich, Conn. He was born in East Haddam Dec. 12, 1816. In school he

A. H. EMMONS.

held the reputation of being the picture-maker of the district. Necessity compelled him to learn the trade of the house-painter. A portrait which he made of a fellow-laborer opened his eyes to the fact that he might be a portrait-painter. He began at once painting miniature portraits on Bristol-board. When twenty years old he married, and, being the only artist in Norwich, found instantly sufficient orders for support, regardless of the fact that the pictures were his first experiments. In 1843 he opened a studio in Hartford, painting both landscapes and portraits, and giving lessons. At the end of five years he accepted a tempting offer from Charles Johnson, Esq., to return to Norwich, where he has since remained. His only absence of any length was during an extended trip through Europe for the purpose of studying the work of the old masters. His work showed great improvement in refinement, taste, and general execution, after his return. Throughout his life in Norwich, Mr. Johnson has proved a firm and valuable friend. Mr. Emmons's native talent is obvious in all of his work, much of which is remarkable for a man who never had an instructor beyond his own observation. He painted a large picture of Rome from the Pincio for Richard Lathers, Esq., of New Rochelle, N.Y., which possessed not only accuracy, but decided artistic ability. He occupies one of the pleasantest studios in the State.

GEORGE W. FLAGG.

A second son of Mayor Flagg of New Haven to follow art was born in that city in 1817. Dunlap speaks of him as a prodigy as long ago as his History was written. Tuckerman enters into a poetical enthusiasm, from which he cannot stoop to the commonplace details : hence there remain only these commonplaces for the present volume to give, in all, a full history of a man who sprang into fame quicker and earlier than any other artist of America. When three years old George W. Flagg was taken by his father to South Carolina, where he remained for ten years. His father objected to an evident passion for drawing; but secretly the boy obtained considerable knowledge of art, and all of his pocket-money was devoted to materials for secret experiments. At last he asserted a determination, and was allowed to take a few lessons of Mr. Bowman, who, when the boy was thirteen, accompanied him to Boston. His career there was simply marvellous. He painted portraits at a fabulous price ; though even so small for his age, that one of the novelties of his life was being held in the lap of one lady while he was painting the portrait of another, and being allowed unlimited license in kissing the pretty sitters, —doubtless a powerful inspiration in portrait-painting. A portrait of Miss Benjamin in particular created a wide excitement in Boston. Unfortunately, even at that early age, he became surfeited with public favor.

While in Boston he received the inestimable advantage of instruction from his uncle Washington Allston, and intimate intercourse with him. At the end of two years he returned to New Haven, where Mr. Jocelyn and Thomas Cole secured for him the patronage of Luman Reed in an arrangement whereby he was to have a regular salary in exchange for the ideal pieces he might paint, his work upon portraits to remain his own. The piece to which he owed this good fortune was "The Ghost-Story," told by an old hag, listened to by a frightened boy. A year later

he sailed for Europe. The first month he spent in England. One of
his first acts was to present a letter to Mr. Constable. The great English
artist, who was then somewhat conceited over his success as champion in
the present French style of landscape, received the boy as a boy, laughed
at the idea of his having studied art, and even told him there was no one
in America able to teach it. American spirit rebelled, and the boy replied
that he had studied under a man who could teach Mr. Constable and all
England. Mr. Constable carried out his opinion by asserting that he had
never even heard the name of Allston, obvious as the lie was, — for Mr.
Allston was then a member with Mr. Constable of the British Royal
Academy, — and supplemented his remarks by saying that it would be

GEORGE W. FLAGG.

better for art were America under the ocean instead of in it. Fired by
this, the boy left with a resolve to show Mr. Constable that he knew something of art, after all. He seized upon a match-seller on the way to his
hotel ; and the result, " The Match-Girl," now in the New-York Historical
Rooms, proved in many respects the masterpiece of the artist's life. Several
in London endeavored to purchase it ; but, though it could not be sold, it
brought the artist orders for the portraits of George Wilds and many
others. He remained abroad but nine months, in which time he painted
with Mr. Healy from live models in Paris, and the old masters in Italy.
When eighteen, he was again established in New Haven. Among other
orders he received was one for the family of Mr. Sheffield, donor of the
Scientific School to Yale College, who paid him two hundred dollars

above his bill, as expression of his satisfaction. Two years later he painted the portrait of Dr. Channing of Boston, which is pronounced the best portrait of his life. At this time he was elected an associate of the National Academy, and in 1851 an academician. He spent four years in New York, and returned to New Haven to paint the "Landing of the Pilgrims" for James Brewster, followed by the "Landing of the Atlantic Cable," "The Good Samaritan," and others. He married when thirty-

"HESTER PRYNNE."—BY GEORGE W. FLAGG.

five, and again removed to New York. During the Rebellion he painted and studied in London, and, returning, remained for a year in New Haven; since which time he has resided in New York. Among the complimentary achievements of his life is the securing of Fanny Kemble as a sitter. She came the first time in a terrific snow-storm, saying she had never broken an engagement in her life. She gave as her reason for never allowing her pictures to become public property, that she was ashamed of her homely mouth; to which the artist gallantly replied, that Nature had doubtless left it unfinished, knowing that she could perfect the work the best.

EDWIN WHITE.

The artist Edwin White, a popular *genre* and historical painter, descended from Elder John White, one of the first settlers on the Connecticut River, just above Hartford, was born in South Hadley, Mass., May 21, 1817. His early life was a gallant struggle to obtain a sound education in art. When eighteen years old he painted for one summer in Longmeadow; coming to Hartford in the fall, and entering the studio of Mr. Hewins as pupil in portraiture. He made rapid progress, and in a few

"THE EVENING-HYMN OF THE HUGUENOT REFUGEES."

months received a commission to paint an original Madonna in Norwalk, Conn. This was followed by others for portraits; and from there he was induced to go to Bridgeport, where he opened a studio. His success was flattering; but, as his critical eye became educated, he was convinced that he yet lacked much. He married in 1841, and, moving at once to New York, placed himself under Professor Smith in practical perspective; attending also lectures in the Medical College to gain a knowledge of anatomy, and studying in the antique and life schools at the National Academy. In 1849 he was made an academician, and in 1850 sailed for Europe, where, in Paris, Düsseldorf, and Florence, he pursued a most thorough course of study. Returning in 1856, he spent the summer in Lakeville, Conn.; while there, receiving the degree of A.M. from Amherst. In the fall he went again to Paris. After an exceedingly happy life, in which he had established a character of the purest and noblest stamp, and a rank in art that was very high, he returned to America in declining health, of which he wrote, " It is the first cross of my life," and died at Saratoga June 7, 1877.

His first attempt at ideal composition was "An Evening at Home," a candle-light scene ; his second, " Country Courtship," now in possession of Professor Weir of Yale College, — a charming little picture, for which his wife and Charles Weir were models. It is a firelight-scene, well painted, and, in point of ability, indicative of the talent displayed in later life. They were painted in Bridgeport, exhibited at the National Academy, and bought by the Art Union. A large picture, "Signing of the Compact on 'The Mayflower,'" is in the Yale Gallery. But the artist's peculiarities of character gave greater excellence to his *genre*-work.

RICHARD WILLIAM HUBBARD.

The President of the Brooklyn Art Association, R. W. Hubbard, born in Middletown, Conn., 1817, has attained a most favorable reputation among the artists of America, as one breathing the atmosphere, both by nature, inheritance, and education, of the highest, truest art. His life and work are of the still waters, running deep, that "many admire, but few may fully penetrate," as one realizes in studying the charming quiet of his paintings, bearing the imprint of Nature's truth in the unostentatious delicacy and refinement characteristic of Nature, but not characteristic of the majority of works of art.

The grandfather of the artist, after honorably serving in the Revolutionary war as Quartermaster-General of Connecticut, entered the West-India trade, establishing himself in Middletown. His father, after several years as shipping-merchant in New York, returned to his native city to become cashier of the Middletown Bank, founded by Col. Hubbard ; which position he held through life. From his mother, who died when he was but eighteen months old, Mr. Hubbard received that delicacy of taste, and love of nature, which characterize him, and which were happily fostered by an aunt, who became his second mother, bringing with her from the Moravian school at Bethlehem, where she was educated, a refined and earnest sympathy for all pertaining to the fine arts. Her home was to him a veritable school of design, exerting a constant, quiet, but powerful influence in favor of the truest and best in art and literature.

After preparing in private and boarding schools, Mr. Hubbard entered Yale College in 1837. The love of art, however, overruled the love of

AN ORIGINAL SKETCH. — BY RICHARD W. HUBBARD.

study; and after receiving a classical education, that has been a source of endless enjoyment to him, he left Yale in 1839 to enter the field in which, thus far, his life has been passed so acceptably and beneficially to others. After a course of study from the antique at the National Academy, he applied for admission as pupil to the studio of Professor Morse. It did not at first appear convenient for Mr. Morse to comply with this request;

and he advised an application to Mr. Allston, then at his home in Cambridge. To this Mr. Allston replied through a long and friendly letter, which Mr. Hubbard still preserves, filled with advice excellently fitted for a young aspirant, closing by once more referring him to Professor Morse. To this second appeal Mr. Morse yielded; and Mr. Hubbard, established in a studio opposite his instructor's, became not only the pupil, but the intimate friend, of the great man. Mr. Hubbard's first bold step in art

AN ORIGINAL SKETCH. — BY RICHARD W. HUBBARD.

was taken at this time in painting from his studio-window the view of Washington Park. In 1840 the young artist sailed for Europe, giving the careful study of an honest, determined ambition to the works of European masters; forming in detail, and still retaining, an especially warm appreciation for the work of Claude Lorraine. Returning to America, he began a course of study under Daniel Huntington. Though in portraiture the artist obtained for himself a careful and thorough education, natural incli-

nation led him at once and finally to the adoption of landscape-painting
for his life's labor; and, removing altogether from Middletown in 1850,
he established himself as a landscape-painter in New-York City, where he
has since remained.   From his position in art and society, he has of course
lived upon terms of the most mutually profitable intimacy with the artists
Huntington, Kensett, Gifford, Church, Hicks, Casilear, and many others,
among whom are many justly the pride of Connecticut as well.   He was
elected an academician of the National Academy of Design in 1858.   Of
the Artists' Fund Society, founded in 1859, he was one of the incorpo-
rators, and was at about the same time elected a member of the Century
Club.

In matters of art Mr. Hubbard is of the very broadest church, — a vital
catholic; and although from the beginning of his study of color in nature
as minute as a Pre-Raphaelite, yet throughout vividly appreciative of tone
and color, space and light.   In fact, one of the sweetest features of the
artist's work is the rare effect of his chiaroscuro.   Nature's most charming aspects are not those in which she is most lavish of her light.   Only
the most passionate and earnest lover of nature among artists discovers
this in his work; but, when discovered, the secret charm enhances all.
That particular phase of nature which has most influenced Mr. Hubbard
in his work is what is known in art as the silvery light, in which this charm
appears, as nowhere else, in its full delicacy and strength and loveliness.
It is noticeable in days when the sunlight softens the decided blue of the
sky into a tender, luminous gray, involving the distances in the same
charming atmosphere, and giving its full value in color to every leaf and
blade of grass.   In such a sky are clouds large and small, of infinitely
varied form, more or less lightened and pervaded by the sun, and capable
of immense range, from the dark storm-cloud to the graceful little islets
quietly anchored in the ocean of light.   Here is a phase of nature that
for ages has tasked the best abilities of artists, and that still retains
resources of subtleties and difficulties amply sufficient to mock the best
efforts of those who are yet to come.   Thirty-six years ago, Mr. Hubbard's attention was first absorbed in the beauty of the silver sky; and
since that time his efforts to catch it upon canvas have been crowned
with a success that will make his name as enduring as his work.   His
paintings are gems of quiet beauty, upon which the highest encomiums
pronounced have been those coming from other artists, which artists
most appreciate.   There is little in them intended to produce a startling
effect; no eccentricity with which one must become acquainted to admire
the whole.   They touch a reverberating sympathy in every honest breast;
while the remarkable harmony in tone, fidelity to truth, and unaffected

simplicity, must always win for them the favor of the most critical. These paintings are the result of slow and careful elaboration; and it is of noticeable interest, that two pieces, prepared for the New-York-Academy Exhibition of 1878, were by many careful observers pronounced the best works of Mr. Hubbard's life.

As a man, the artist thoroughly partakes of the tenor of his work. Connecticut proudly claims him as her son.

JOHN F. KENSETT.

The father of one of the greatest, though perhaps not among the most prominent artists in America, came to this country from England in 1812. He had been a distinguished engraver of Hampton Court. His son, John F. Kensett, born in Cheshire, Conn., March 22, 1818, learned after him the engraver's trade, completing his study under his uncle Alfred Daggett of New Haven, his mother being grand-daughter of President Daggett of Yale College. At that early age he was considered such a proficient workman, that he was immediately secured by the American Bank-Note Company, and moved to New York.

The inspiration of art was not satisfied. Kensett was an intimate friend of Rossiter and several other artists, and in their studios he began with experiments destined finally to resolve into an almost unexcelled victory. In a little over two years he left for Europe to see and study art in company with Messrs. Durand, Casilear, and Rossiter. It opened a new world to him. He carefully studied English landscape and French and German art with Henry Champney, and walked through Switzerland with George W. Curtis and a small party, making the most of every opportunity. They reached Rome in November, 1845. At that time there were in Rome, among the resident American artists, Thomas Crawford, Luther Terry, and H. K. Brown; among the students, George Baker, E. Terry, Thomas Hicks, T. McClurg, and Stevenson the sculptor. William Story, C. Perkins, George Curtis, and others, were also living in Rome at the time. Leutze had just left for America. In this inspiring society Mr. Kensett began his study of art in Rome with full vigor and enthusiasm. His first annoyance was in the non-appearance of his baggage, which he had sent before him, but which did not appear for over two months. He was not travelling with a purse capable of overcoming any and all obstacles at that early day in his afterward brilliant career, and experienced no little inconvenience in stretching out the endurance of the old clothes till they should be relieved by the recruits already enlisted, but slow to appear. The next difficulty lay in a severe attack of inflammatory rheumatism, that prostrated him for several weeks during his first winter. He found a valuable friend in Thomas Hicks, however; rooming, eating, working with him through his entire life in Rome; knowing him, doubtless, as the same warm-hearted, true-hearted man that he is to-day.

In June Mr. Kensett, in a party of four artists, — Messrs. Hicks, Boujac, and S. A. Smith, — went on a summer's sketching trip through South Italy. On the 1st of August, reaching an isolated village where they proposed stopping a fortnight, they sent back their donkeys, cutting off their only mode of retreat, and, the inn being closed for want of custom, rented the upper story of the largest, cleanest house in town; but were driven sleepless from their beds by hosts of the little bed-lovers of Southern Italy. In the morning they found every inhabitant of the place anxious to rob them of any thing or every thing. While two stood guard, two hunted for donkeys to take them away. Succeeding at last, they were literally stoned from the village by the inhabitants, angry at the loss of their expected profits. After all, they had one package stolen. This, proving to possess nothing of value, was returned in a few days with a humble request for a reward. At their next start the driver failed to furnish the baggage-mule engaged. They protested in vain; but, as they were about to start, the driver's wife appeared, and on her head and shoulders took the entire baggage of the company, trudging on with the *other* mules, while her husband with a long whip walked behind to keep his caravan in motion. It was one of the rare instances in Mr. Kensett's life when he thoroughly lost his temper. They returned to Rome in October, 1846; and Mr. Kensett continued his study with most satisfactory and productive diligence until August, 1847, when he left for Venice for a month; thence through Germany again with Mr. Curtis, and back to America, where he established himself in New York.

When he reached Rome, as an artist he was in an unfortunate plight. He had studied the French styles, and copied them. He had studied the German styles, and copied them. He had given up his own originality altogether; and his work was a complete mannerism, the French and German schools jumbled. Discovering his error, his study in Rome became, not one of Roman art, but of individuality, which should embrace the virtues of all, yet express the characteristics of none. This individuality is the charm of all of his later work.

In Rome Mr. Kensett was very poor, and, in the results of his career from beginning to end, is a wonderful example of the possibilities before an artist. He left six hundred studies, sketches, and finished pictures, in his studio, when he died; and being sold at auction in March, 1873, they brought over a hundred and fifty thousand dollars to add to an already ample fortune, which, being a bachelor, he left unreservedly to his mother. It was the most remarkable sale upon record in America. It was held in the large hall of the Young Men's Christian Association Building, New-York City, and occupied six evenings. J. F. Kensett possessed in Mr. Oliphant a valuable and life-long friend, to whom and Vincent Colyer is due, in some degree, the success of the auction. His best two pictures, the " Genesee River " and " Lake George," were purchased by the Corcoran Gallery, in opposition to David Dows of New York, owner of " The Heart of the Andes," — as great a compliment as could well have been bestowed upon their worth. The price paid (six thousand dollars) has in a few instances been exceeded in America ; but the state of the times, and the value of money comparatively, render them almost the highest original-cost pictures of American painting.

John F. Kensett was noted through art-circles as the beginner's friend. The struggles against poverty in his early life gave him a keen appreciation of how early struggles might be relieved. He was a short, plethoric man, remarkably even in temperament, and quiet in manner. As a consequence, he was one of the most popular artists of the country, so far as he was truly known. He said but little ; but his influence was widely felt. He was, if a fault were visible, over-conscientious with his own work, and over-charitable with the work of others. He was foremost in every thing charitable, and an efficient laborer. He was among the first supporters of the Artists' Fund, of which he was for some time president. Many an artist gaining prominence and fame to-day remembers with affection a word or an act of encouragement from him at a time when it may have been much needed. A single example will suffice. Learning that an artist struggling against many obstacles had reached a chasm that threatened seriously to interrupt his progress unless bridged for him in some way by a helping hand, he carelessly entered the studio, making comments in his happy style upon the merits and demerits of the young man's work. He praised a nearly completed canvas, and offered the painter three hundred dollars for it. The bridge was instantly constructed, and the picture finished with a zest that made a far better work of it than it could otherwise have been.

As an artist, Mr. Kensett was doubtless superior to many whose reputation stood higher than his own. His " Morning on the Lake," for instance, is imbued with a poetic feeling and quiet beauty, for the proper conveyance of which words are altogether an inadequate vehicle. Characteristically, his works could find expression only in themselves. If there were a mannerism, it was such a charming manner as to be forgotten even by the critics. They are replete with a style of beauty possessed by few other paintings. In 1848 they won for the author election as an academician. He has been particularly lauded by the pre-Raphaelites for the literal minuteness in his work upon mosses, rocky ledges, dripping stones, and mouldy lichens, almost after the Flemish painters.

During the riots in New York, Mr. Kensett proved himself as bold in action as in art. He returned to Connecticut for the last summer of his life, having with Vincent Colyer purchased a part of Contentment Island, a mile from Darien. Mr. Colyer's wife was drowned in the fall; and Mr. Kensett, in expending every possible energy to recover the body, contracted a severe cold, which terminated in an attack of pneumonia. He had apparently recovered from this, and had already walked out, when on Saturday noon a servant came to his studio-door in the Young Men's Christian Association Building, New-York City, and asked if his lunch should be brought up. He answered "Yes," and went on with his work. Returning with the lunch, the servant found him sitting on a sofa, dead, Dec. 14, 1872. The body was first placed in the Second-street vault, and afterward removed to Greenwood.

JOHN DURRIE.

In 1818 John Durrie was born in Hartford. He and a younger brother, George H. Durrie, entered the field of art together, beginning study under Nathaniel Jocelyn in New Haven. John Durrie turned his attention at once to portraiture and still-life, to which branches he has given his chief exertions, fulfilling the sanguine hopes of many friends. He has passed most of his life, thus far, in New Haven, and in the course of it has also produced some very acceptable landscapes. He has all his life been an ardent devotee, but not an enthusiast in art, which his work indicates.

THOMAS P. ROSSITER.

A singular composition, making up an artist of high rank, born in New Haven Sept. 29, 1818, appeared in the person of Thomas P. Rossiter. As a lad he was taken to Winsted, and apprenticed to a Mr. Boyd; but at eighteen he appeared in Mr. Jocelyn's studio, saying he intended to make an artist of himself, and wanted help. For two years he studied there, then opened a studio of his own, as portrait, figure, landscape, and, indeed, every kind of a painter. In two years he sailed for Europe with Messrs. Durand, Kensett, and Casilear. He enjoyed abroad the very great privilege of sketching through Switzerland with Thomas Cole, and a life of five years in Italy. In 1851 he opened a studio in New York. Two years later he again went abroad, returning in 1856, when he began work upon "The Merchant Princes of America" on an order from William Wright, spoken of elsewhere. His collection (due to his characteristic impetuosity) was the only one of the four ever finished, and now hangs in the Young Men's Christian Association Rooms, New York. In 1860 he purchased and moved into a beautiful villa opposite West Point, where he died at the age of fifty, five years before his life-friend Kensett.

As an artist Mr. Rossiter was not a complete success, nor yet by any means a failure. He had much ability in color, and ready skill in catching a likeness. But in drawing he was more deficient. Many of his larger pictures he sent about the country on exhibition : in fact, his success was partially due to the energy with which he kept himself before the public. In 1840 he was recognized by the National Academy as an associate, and in 1849 made an academician. He certainly played an important part in his department. His pictures were generally large, and in gay colors, but, instead of improving, bore more evidence of careless-ness, toward the end of his life. He doubtless had great talent, — too great, perhaps ; at least, an energy that drove his ability beyond its power, to speak literally. His smaller pictures are, many of them, exquisite gems ; but the larger ones are invariably confused. The number of sacred and historical subjects which he treated on large canvases is simply amazing. It is absolutely impossible that they did him even a meagre justice. An applicable criticism comes to mind in an anecdote equally characteristic of both parties. Rossiter asked Kensett to criticise an immense landscape ; and, to counterbalance the fault found with it, Rossi-ter explained, "But you must remember, the whole thing was painted in a single day ; " when Kensett quietly asked, "Why didn't you take two?" Had Rossiter taken two days for one in his larger works, the world would have known him to-day as a master among American artists. He was social, generous, remarkably handsome, and talented in literature as well as art. He died suddenly at his home on the Hudson, leaving, be-sides his paintings, an unpublished but exceedingly interesting work on the legends of the Catskills.

FREDERIC STILES JEWETT.

The marine-painter F. S. Jewett was born in Simsbury, Conn., Feb. 26, 1819. When sixteen he entered a whaler, on which he passed two years before the mast, in the South-Pacific and Indian Oceans. Returning, he began a literary life ; moving to the West Indies when twenty-two, where he married. In various capacities he proved himself an excellent writer. Only the last seven years of his life were devoted entirely to art. He visited Europe, and studied under the best French and English teachers. He was strictly a marine-painter; and his work had the merit of faithfulness often wanting in the marine-painting of the day, he having known the sea as a sailor before knowing it as an artist. Wide experience had made him a good judge of men, and during his art-life he entered warmly into politics in Connecticut. Artist-life, however, was not an afterthought, but had been foreshadowed in the schoolboy's propensity for picture-making, and an acknowledged ambition, while other things prevented its fulfilment. Much of his time while connected with the city government of Hartford was occupied in designing for and making Bushnell Park. Mr. Jewett died in Cleveland, O., Dec. 26, 1864, a growing man in art, with remarkable talent. He imitated Turner, possessing a strong admiration for him; but this did not prevent a visible originality. One of his best pieces hangs in the Wadsworth Athenæum.

CHARLES LANMAN.

The well-known author and artist Charles Lanman cannot well be omitted in a history of art in Connecticut; for, though born in Michigan

CHARLES LANMAN.

(June 14, 1819), his father Charles James, and grandfather James Lanman, were men of mark in Norwich, Conn. He received his education at the

Plainfield Academy and in Norwich, where his sister still resides, and where, for a long time, was the home of his family. In 1835 he became clerk in an East-India house in New York, and while in that capacity commenced the study of art. In 1845 he began his life as a writer, being successively connected in editorial capacity with several of the leading journals of the day, still continuing his art-work. He was one of the first writers in New York to devote elaborate attention to home art. This was so happily appreciated, that, in return, Mr. Lanman's walls were decorated with gifts from many of the leading artists. He has visited in sketching-trips every State east of the Rocky Mountains, and was the first to

"A DESERTED HOUSE." — BY CHARLES LANMAN.

produce upon canvas the beauties of many locations now frequented by artists. Many of these sketches have since been published in "The London Illustrated News" and American magazines, as well as in his own volumes. He has held many posts of literary honor under the government, and was private secretary to Daniel Webster. He has also been American correspondent for "The London Illustrated News" and "London Athenæum." As an author Mr. Lanman's reputation is well known. His works of history, geography, biography, adventure, &c., have had extensive circulation, and many have been republished in England. Also soon forthcoming are three works, — "Hap-hazard

Personalities," "Novelties of American Character," and "Evenings in My Library," — in all of which he has gathered much interesting art-matter.

In 1847 he was elected an associate of the National Academy. Never having devoted more than leisure time to art, he has learned to work rapidly. His last and largest picture, five feet long, a "View of Fieziyama, Japan," was painted in two weeks, before breakfast. It was purchased by the Japanese Government. Miss Caulkins's "History of Norwich" was illustrated by Mr. Lanman. In 1871 he was appointed American secretary of the Japanese Legation in Washington; which position he still occupies, residing in Georgetown, D.C.

EDWARD W. NICHOLS,

A New-Hampshire lawyer, born in Orford April 23, 1819, preferring art to law, changed his profession; and after studying landscape-painting in New York with Cropsey in 1848, and abroad in 1853, he sketched and painted to some extent about Hartford, where he married. He died in Peekskill, on the Hudson, Sept. 20, 1871. E. W. Wells of Hartford has several of his pictures. They are full of feeling, and well executed.

JARED B. FLAGG.

The third artist-son of Mayor Flagg of New Haven, Jared B. Flagg, was born in that city in 1820. The oldest son, though practising art, was in the naval service. The second, George W., the mayor had been unable to restrain from art; but, having a financially low opinion of the profession, he facetiously remarked that "one vagabond in a family was enough," and to prevent another, so soon as Jared appeared discontented with school-life, placed him as clerk in a store. It was not long, however, before the drudgery became irksome, and the boy insisted upon studying art under his brother. Six months later he went with him upon his second trip to Boston, where both enjoyed the advantages of association with their uncle Washington Allston. At seventeen Jared Flagg began independent portrait-painting, and two years later settled in Hartford, where he remained for ten years. The portrait of Dr. Robbins, now in the Historical Rooms, was painted at this time, and those of several of the governors. A week after opening his studio he received an order for the portrait of Judge Hitchcock, that now hangs in the Alumni Hall at Yale. Shortly after settling in Hartford the artist married Miss Sarah Montague, a lady of rare beauty, who died two years and six months after, leaving a son, the present artist Montague Flagg. This affliction resulted in a decision on the part of the artist to enter the ministry. He received but twenty-five dollars for pictures that to-day bring him five hundred, and hence was obliged to devote incessant labor to his profession for support, giving only his evenings to study. When twenty-eight he married again, and moved to Brooklyn, N.Y., where, in 1849, the artist C. N. Flagg was born. During his first year in New York he painted a scene from "Measure for Measure," — "Angelo and Isabella," — which he exhibited at the National Academy, and was elected an academician. In 1852 he completed his preparatory studies, passed the examination for the Episcopal ministry, and in 1854 was settled in Birmingham, Conn. In nine months he

JARED B. FLAGG.

accepted an invitation to succeed Dr. Vinton in Grace Church, Brooklyn Heights, where he remained through the longest rectorship of the parish. The ill health of his wife necessitated his removal; when, after six months in Minnesota, he again opened a studio in New Haven. In 1866 Columbia College conferred upon him the degree of "D.D." In 1861 he received the "A.M." from New Haven. In 1869 he married again, in Paris, the daughter of Ex-Congressman Bond, a lady of many charming qualities. From 1870 to 1873 he painted in New Haven, and, since that date, has resided in New York. Portraiture has been his profession, in which he has a high reputation. His ideal pieces express refinement, good taste, a faithful feeling for color, and are invariably pleasing. His constant occupation at present indicates a flattering popularity.

GEORGE H. DURRIE.

A younger brother of John Durrie, George Henry, was born in New Haven June 6, 1820. In his favorite branch, the delineation of pastoral and snow scenes, he was among the first painters of his day in the country. In boyhood he developed a remarkably frank and gentle disposition, which was a characteristic of his life : at the same time, love of the beautiful, and love of art, appeared very strongly fixed in his nature. When twenty-one, having studied for two years with Mr. Jocelyn, he

GEORGE H. DURRIE.

married Miss Sarah A. Perkins, a most estimable lady, and opened a studio in New Haven. With the exception of a few months very successfully passed in Monmouth County, N.J., under the influential patronage of Judge Lawrence, the most of his work was done in New Haven. He began with portrait-painting, the legitimate result of his education, but soon turned his attention almost wholly to landscape. He carefully looked at nature ; and his studies of rocks, barks, lichens, and moss, are of particular interest, being finished with the most faithful minuteness. At a State fair in New Haven, some of Mr. Durrie's work obtained the gold medal, as the finest in the art department. His farm-scenes and snow-scenes were by far his best : his groupings of animals were always pleasing and artistic. One of his well-executed works, "Winter in the Country," was purchased by the Yale Art School after his death, and is on exhibition in the gallery.

Mr. Durrie died in 1863, in the growing-time of life. He was an expert in music as well as art, and his studio was a model of grace and refinement. He well earned for himself the popular distinction of the "New-England Farm-scene Painter."

RALPH ISHAM.

A portrait and landscape painter, Ralph Isham, born about 1820, took charge of the Wadsworth Athenæum Gallery when it was first opened. He was of a wretchedly morbid, dyspeptic disposition ; but withal his work displays much originality, force, and good taste. This is the more surprising, as his first instruction (probably his only instruction) in art came through his eyes from the pictures about him in the gallery. He was an intimate friend of Mr. Church and Mr. Bartholomew ; and for years an old rock on Talcott Mountain, near Hartford, bore the names of Church, Isham, Emmons, and Bartholomew, painted when the artists were upon a sketching-trip in 1845. He was naturally fault-finding with all works of art, especially his own ; and his nervous temperament rendered it difficult for him to meet with satisfactory success in portrait-painting : hence his work is chiefly landscape. One of his pieces in the Wadsworth Gallery, and another owned by the late James B. Hosmer of Hartford, are exceptionally well drawn, delicate in gradations, and with a fine, sensitive, æsthetic taste. He was a man of strong sentiment and religious faith, but at one time fulfilled a vow not to enter a church for a year, explaining that he found himself becoming so indifferent to the privilege, that he was trying if abstinence would not renew a proper enjoyment. Mr. Isham died early in life, before any of the ambitions and powers he possessed were sufficiently developed to form a judgment upon them.

GEORGE A. BAKER.

George A. Baker has lived in Darien since 1866 in a quaint old mansion built in the substantial, liberal style of a half-century ago. As one of the most remarkable portrait-painters of America, though born in New York, 1821, it is but just to the State that we claim his influence, both for the present and the future, upon her art-history. He was an artist born and bred. His father was an artist before him, of excellent ideas and exceptional talents ; and, when only sixteen, he entered the profession as a miniature-portrait painter so successfully, that during the first year he painted one hundred and forty portraits, receiving five dollars each.   Upon this native ability he has placed years of patient study, which together have made the so nearly perfect artist.   During seven years that he painted portraits in miniature, he studied in the antique and life schools in the National Academy ; then sailed for Europe for the purpose of perfecting himself in oil-painting.   A brief sketch of his early achievements is contained in Mr. Tuckerman's book on artists.   With the exception of the very first of his work in oil, he has painted nothing but portraits, often having orders for two years in advance.   In 1851 he was made an academician ; and though a life-sufferer from neuralgia, and seriously interrupted by trouble with his eyes, the quantity of the work he has performed, as well as its quality, is truly astonishing.   Two portraits, just completed, of his wife and daughter, are by good judges pronounced the best work of his life.   In the painting of female heads, and children, he is particularly felicitous.   He is an unassuming gentleman, of the highest refinement and intelligence ; and partaking of this, perhaps, his portraits of men are sometimes criticised as lacking in masculine vigor.   He has painted an excellent portrait of the daughter of the late Joseph Church of Hartford, sister of the artist.

A well-known artist and writer, in a letter concerning Mr. Baker, says, "One secret of his great success is the concentration of all his powers upon the one specialty of *portrait-painting*.   Like Doré, the great French artist, ' he builds no villas ; ' he never touches politics, philanthropy, or literature.   Art, and portrait-painting the only art, occupies all of his working hours."

JULIUS THEODORE BUSCH.

Those interested in matters pertaining to art or music in Hartford from 1850 to 1860 will remember Mr. Julius Busch, — a man of unusually small figure, brown hair, and sandy beard, quiet and undemonstrative, always following diligently the occupation of the hour.   He was born in Dresden, Germany, in 1821, and received a complete education in the Dresden Academy.   He came to Hartford in 1850, and opened a studio, which he occupied for eight years, with the exception of a trip which he made to Germany in 1855.   His forte was teaching ; and he was, during the last of his life in Hartford, favored with many students in drawing, besides teaching large classes in the New-Britain Normal School, the Hartford Female Seminary, the Deaf and Dumb Asylum, and the High School.   His knowledge of art, and his mastery of the rules and laws, were exceptional.   His criticisms and directions to pupils were always clear, precise, and valuable. His inimitable manner of giving these directions can never be forgotten by any who ever sat under his instruction. Probably from want of sufficient time, his larger pictures fail of attaining that excellence which his knowledge and judgment seemed to render possible. His smaller works are better ; an Oriental scene, for instance, and " An Indian Girl going over the Falls," — an excellent bit of color. His knowledge of art covered a wide field ; and he has left some charming water-colors, pen-and-ink, India-ink, and crayon drawings. An enthusiast in art, his great success as a teacher lay in imparting to the pupil the same enthusiasm. Many of the present artists whose names do honor to the history of Connecticut's art were pupils under Mr. Busch.

He was exceedingly poor during the first of his art-life in Hartford, but, by patient, unremitting labor, won for himself the respect and support of those about him. In 1854 he married Miss Howe of Hartford, a sister of the late E. G. Howe.

Mr. Busch was as well informed in music as in art, and for several years sang in the choir of the Centre Church. By birth and education he was a Lutheran ; but sitting continually under the preaching of Dr. Hawes induced him to change his views to some extent, and he was baptized, and admitted to the Centre Church on profession of faith. Twice he returned to Germany to execute orders ; and when last crossing the ocean, in 1858, from Germany, was on board the Hamburg steamer " Austria," burned and lost at sea.

THEODORE S. SPERRY.

Dr. T. S. Sperry was born in Bozrahville, Conn., 1822. His father was a physician ; and he followed his profession, graduating in Boston. He was at one time professor of surgery and botany in the New-York Metropolitan College. Ever an ardent lover of art, in 1844 he made his first attempt in the use of colors, and with such success, that at first his leisure time, and later in life nearly all of his time, was devoted to painting. Landscape was the branch to which he devoted the most of his energy ; and his scenes from about the Connecticut Valley, and picturesque landscapes in the neighborhood of Hartford, where he resided, invariably possessed a pleasing freshness, indicative of a sympathy with nature very commendable. Dr. Sperry met with his death in a very unfortunate manner while completing some scenery-work in Allyn Hall left undone by the death of E. Paul Barnes. He stepped backward to examine his work, and fell through a trap nearly sixty feet to the stage below.

EDWARD SHEFFIELD BARTHOLOMEW.

The most tragic, most heroic, most victorious, and at once most unsatisfactory life that artist ever lived was perhaps the life of Edward Bartholomew. He was born in Colchester, Conn., in 1822. His early life was the precise reverse of his later years. His home in the quiet village was as quiet as the village, and his time as devoid of jarring antagonism. His first fifteen years were passed there, a common-school education obtained, and a reputation gained of being a pleasant, social, and remarkably intelligent and affectionate child. When he was fifteen, and his father, Abial L. Bartholomew, moved to Hartford with his family, Edward

EDWARD SHEFFIELD BARTHOLOMEW. — FROM A PEN-SKETCH BY HIMSELF.

accepted reluctantly the necessity of breaking these cords of sympathy and unity. He was naturally and always sensitive; but there had been little in his early surroundings to interfere with the even course of nature. On arriving in Hartford the scene altogether changed. Naturally quiet and thoughtful, he became reserved and apparently sullen, averse to testing the confidence of his fellows, and unsympathetic so far as outward appearance was concerned. It grew upon him year by year, as one cause and another conspired to create opposition to his course in the minds of those with whom he came in contact. He wrote to a friend from Rome, long afterward, "I have never been able to overcome my repugnance at meeting strangers, occasioned by my first impressions of the world in Hartford." An almost inevitable accompaniment to such a disposition is impetuosity in judgment, and quick temper. Those who remember Edward Bartholomew in early life, before in hard battles he had become master of himself, remember him as rash, and easily enraged. With the few who were allowed to enter the inner circle of his life, such moments are forgotten in the bitter repentance that always came after. An intimate friend writes of him, "I have known Edward many times to regret for weeks, with the most vivid remorse, the trivial outburst for a moment of the temper he struggled so valiantly to crush." So much for the incidental characteristics that exerted their influence over his future.

Soon after settling in Hartford he was apprenticed to a bookbinder, and to satisfy his friends, and from the inevitable necessity of doing something, gave every energy to the task of fitting himself for that trade. It was utterly useless, however. His next trial was dentistry in the office of Dr. Crane. He held to this by force of a strong will for four years, against the objections which nature raised. The reasons for these objections were a mystery; and probably none more than he regretted it when again that destiny which shapes our ends literally drove him from this second trial, leaving him, as he afterward jestingly said, "a vagabond, whose only trade was staring at pictures." It was with more of an idea of ridding himself of his present surroundings, in which he considered himself a "vagabond," than with any thought of becoming an artist, that he went to New York and studied for a year in the antique and life schools in the National Academy of Design. He supported himself during the year by a resort to his knowledge of dentistry, and returned to Hartford with simply a crayon head of Homer. It was admirably executed, no doubt; but, when some one suggested it to the artist, he simply replied, "Any fool could do it after studying for a year." When twenty-three, fortune placed him in charge of the Wadsworth Gallery. This was a step of progress. At this time two of the few friendships of his life were formed with the artists F. E. Church and Ralph Isham, that served to strengthen the influences.

In his leisure hours he indulged a passion for drawing, that, in the practical view he had taken of life, had been voluntarily disregarded as an unprofitable accomplishment. He made copies of figures on Etruscan vases, of engravings of the cartoons of Raphael, and, in black and white, of some of the paintings.

When only sixteen he had painted several pieces: hence it was not in entire ignorance either of drawing or color that he turned his attention to easel and palette, and he was soon at work upon a large picture. In this work, inconsistent with all previous indications, he possessed in an extraordinary degree that important quality, perseverance. While thus occupied, he suddenly discovered that he was unable to tell red from green. In unutterable chagrin he took a large brush filled with paint, and drew 'it mercilessly over the picture. Then he kicked the easel, canvas and all, to the end of the room, and threw his palette and brushes after the wreck.

As a schoolboy, Edward Bartholomew had exhibited a passion for modelling in clay. After giving up the art of painting, he was left involuntarily to turn to that which all his life had been waiting for him. Securing a piece of marble, he attempted a medallion head of Mrs. Sigourney. This he did in the utmost secrecy, fearing even to allow his left hand to know what his right was doing, lest another disappointment might be in store for him. He was working upon a block of marble wholly unfit for the purpose. He had simply a furniture-hammer, and a file for a chisel, when discovered by J. G. Batterson, Esq., who sent him a proper piece of marble, a mallet, and complete set of tools; and the result, in the medallion of the authoress now on exhibition in the Bartholomew Collection, was unquestionably astonishing. The result of his next trial was "Flora," still pronounced an exquisite work; and with it his true life may be said to have begun. James B. Hosmer, the late venerable patriarch of Hartford, was his first live model, sitting for him at the earnest request of the artist, that he might try his next experiment with a friendly face, catching a likeness from life.

Mr. Bartholomew now went again to New York, to attend anatomical lectures by Dr. Watts, preparatory to going to Italy to study.

While occupying a temporary studio in the University Building, New York, his washerwoman brought his clothes, having left them, as he discovered, in the room with a small-pox patient. He directed her to wash them again; and, to her negligence and dishonesty in not obeying, the world must charge a terrible blow that virtually wrecked one of the greatest promises that were ever couched in an aspiring artist. What he did achieve, great as it was, is evidently but the shadow of what he would have accomplished in health and strength. The disease, having spent its fury upon him, settled in his hip, leaving him a cripple for life, with a previously vigorous constitution sadly broken down.

Mr. Bartholomew was a remarkably handsome man. He was tall, erect, and strong. He had coal-black hair, and black, flashing eyes. His cheeks were red, his nose decidedly Roman; and his head rested with haughty, fearless grace upon his shoulders. He was the personification of an artist. In winter he wore a long black cloak thrown about his shoulders, that fairly completed the picture. He was sensitive, brave, and proud. To reduce such a man to the pale convalescent from small-pox, and force him to bend to crutches, is a blow such as few could have received without bitter disapproval. But he had no idea of abandoning art; and, after spending the summer testing every means for recovery, he started in the early winter of 1850, on crutches, for the Eternal City of the Italians, in an Italian vessel poorly fitted for the accommodation of an invalid. The misery he endured was so great, that, sighting France, he was, at his earnest request, allowed to land, and make the best of his way to Rome. The third day after his arrival in Rome, from this long season of hardships that justly earned for him a recreation, he was found by a friend, almost too busy to speak, working on the model of his "Blind Homer led by his Daughter," in his first studio on the Piazza di Mignonelli.

His first year he spent under the instruction of Sig. Giorgio Ferero, giving his principal attention to bass-relief. He achieved such rapid success in this branch, that Ferero induced him to visit Greece in order to study there the perfection of the art; and the following summer he made an extended trip through the East in pursuit of this and other ends.

The Hon. Henry C. Deming of Hartford, delivering a lecture on Mr. Bartholomew shortly after his death, quoted from a letter by a visitor at Mr. Bartholomew's studio: "I was astonished at the *variety* also in the Bartholomew studio. But, when I came to look over his portfolios, I found a key to the knowledge he shows. I found sketches of scenery and figures through Italy, Greece, Turkey, Syria, Palestine, and Egypt; crayon-portraits of the crowned heads of a dozen different nations; elaborate anatomical and beautiful architectural drawings; temples of Pæstum, Athens, Asia Minor, Holy Land, and the Nile. And these are but items of the mass of information stored in the artist's brain and his portfolios."

In one of many exceedingly interesting letters written by the artist, he says of himself, "I am like one whose youth and buoyancy is burned out by premature age and decay. I can see no relief. Contentment and happiness are not my lot. Happiness I crave; but contentment would only increase my misery. Who wishes for contentment? If contented, I should have nothing to live for or to strive after; no ambition, no excitement. I might as well be a stone. Infinitely better if hewn into a statue! To become contented is drinking of the waters of oblivion. Let me never taste of either." Later in the same letter he says, "I am now at work upon my 'Ganymede' and 'Eagle of Jupiter.' Twelve hours at least out of every twenty-four are spent upon them. They haunt me nights to such a degree, that I sometimes think I shall go mad. But my courage is as good as ever, and my determination much greater. If poverty keep the upper hand, I will work in a garret; but my earnestness for truth and excellence shall strike a blow in art which shall be felt."

His greatest work was certainly "Eve Repentant," and the bass-relief groups for the pedestal, without a characteristic fault, and open to criticism only where blunders from inexperience may be found, that time and study would surely have overcome. It is unfortunate for Hartford that the original of this masterpiece should be owned in Philadelphia, and only a laborer's copy of the artist's model possessed in the Bartholomew Collection. However, many thanks are due to the generosity and energy of James B. Hosmer, J. G. Batterson, J. W. Stancliff, and others, that so much has been secured which would otherwise have been entirely lost to the city that owned the author as her prodigy. The first copy, bearing the artist's own work in the finish, had already been sent to Philadelphia when Mr. Batterson arrived in Rome, after Bartholomew's death; but the model was left, and the workmen who had cut the first statue under the master's direction and criticism were not too widely scattered to be brought together again for another endeavor. Their work was well done, the circumstances considered; but the value of the author's immediate attention with every stroke, and especially his careful eye, and sensitive desire for the perfection of his work as it approaches completion, cannot be over-estimated. This care the copy in the Wadsworth Athenæum lacks; and certain of the last, most delicate, most artistic touches to be found in the first are wanting in the second. It is, however, a treasure that cannot be too highly prized, translating the thought, if not with the exquisite delicacy of the sculptor, at least with his individuality of conception and design. The statue is large life-size, and at first sight may strike the observer as being somewhat out of proportion, the lower limbs, and especially the ankles, appearing over-large: but, according to the strict laws of proportion, the body is correct; and the national characteristics in face and figure of every model must be considered, accounting for many peculiarities that might otherwise be faults.

The "Eve" sits upon an irregular rock: at her feet lies an apple; about the base of the rock is coiled the serpent; while the half-finished apron of leaves lies forgotten in her lap. The whole rests on an octangular pedestal. This pedestal bears the bass-reliefs, the original models for which are owned by the Yale Art School, representing scenes in and out of the first garden before and after the first temptation. These bass-reliefs are, if any thing, more valuable specimens of the artist's work than even the principal figure.

This work, however, should not be allowed to overshadow the graces of the rest. The following list of the more prominent among them is

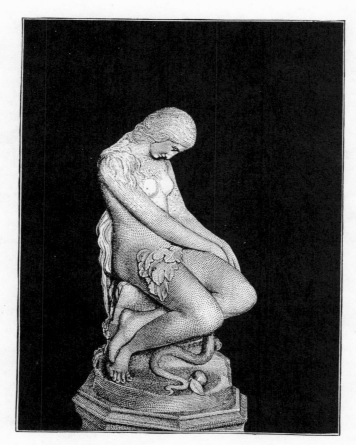

"EVE REPENTANT," BY E. S. BARTHOLOMEW.

copied: "Calypso," "Sappho," "Campagna," "Genius of Music," "Genius of Painting," "Shepherd Boy," "Infant Pan and the Wizards," "Ruth and Naomi," or "Youth and Old Age," "Ganymede" and the "Eagle of Jupiter," "Genevieve," "Homer and his Daughter," "The Evening Star," "Washington," besides many others, and much ornamental work upon monuments, and copies made of several of the best designs. Yet his work was just begun. His individual merit, evident in all of his work, was an intuitive perception of the strongest and most artesque aspect of the theme in hand, and a clear delineation of the idea as it was thus presented.

Twice after his establishment in Rome he returned to Hartford for a short visit, each time being overloaded with orders. His celebrity had reached such a point, that upon the second visit a very unusual token of public opinion was tendered by the people of Hartford in the shape of a grand dinner given to the two great representatives and intimate friends Bartholomew and Church.

Few if any of the orders received upon this visit were even begun in marble. His death, occurring when it did, is the strangest, most unreconcilable incident of his life. The stilling of his hand, the hushing of his mallet, the silencing of his brain in death, at the moment when enthusiasm and inspiration were rapidly carrying him to great achievements, are incomprehensible providences that must always remain past finding out. He had suffered, though not severely, for several weeks, almost immediately after his return from America; and was persistently urged by the physician under whose care he had placed himself to leave for Naples, in the hope of benefit from the change. He had been but a short time in Naples when he was prostrated by an alarming increase of the trouble in his throat. After a doubtful struggle for life he rallied, and had nearly recovered from the disease as seated in his throat, when his system, already in a precarious condition as the result of overwork (indeed, he had never been well since his partial recovery from the small-pox), suffered a general relapse, which ended in his forfeiture of life. Mr. Osgood, an artist well known in Hartford fifty years ago, was with him when he died.

On the announcement of his death, a sum of money was immediately raised in Hartford, and J. G. Batterson intrusted to act for the subscribers in securing the casts and any works that might be left in his studio, for constant exhibition in the Athenæum, in the room where he had cut his first marble.

Only a short time before his death, which occurred May, 1858, while talking with a friend, in the Protestant cemetery at Naples, of the warm south-western knoll, catching the breezes from Africa and the ocean, and illuminated by the sun in its most glowing setting, he exclaimed, "What a lovely spot! If I die in Italy, I hope I may be buried there." It was a strange sequel to that wish, that so soon others strolling over that ever-sunny knoll should find a new tomb touched by the red glow of the Mediterranean twilight, and should read upon the monument that marked it, —

"𝔖𝔞𝔠𝔯𝔢𝔡 𝔱𝔬 𝔱𝔥𝔢 𝔐𝔢𝔪𝔬𝔯𝔶

OF

EDWARD SHEFFIELD BARTHOLOMEW."

THE BARTHOLOMEW GRAVE IN NAPLES.

CHARLES DE WOLF BROWNELL.

The artist Brownell, born in Providence in 1822, was brought to East Hartford when two years old. He grew up in Connecticut, and thoroughly identified himself in his art-life with the State. From 1824 to 1860 his home remained in East Hartford. The first nineteen years were of ordinary study and preparation for the bar. The principal indications of the boyhood which have proved of greatest value in forming the character of the man were fearlessness, ardent affection, scrupulous faithfulness. On several occasions this ambition to exceed rather than fall short of duty has brought upon him the serious results of overtaxed health.

He carried into his study of law the same energy, and was admitted to the bar in 1843. He practised in Hartford for ten years, except three winters spent at the South for his health. In 1853, while depressed by the effects of a severe attack of congestion of the lungs, he fell into a moralizing mood. The conclusion of the matter was a call upon Henry

Bryant, with the declaration that he could not be an honest man and be a successful lawyer, and was ready to look at the propriety of becoming a landscape-painter, for which he had always possessed a strong ambition. The talent and taste were inherited from his mother, who was an excellent artist, though not a professional painter. The sacrifice of the law was made at no small cost of courage; for a good income at the bar is not with impunity exchangeable for an artist's livelihood. In Mr. Brownell's brother, Henry Howard, the poet, he found his most ardent supporter. His first instruction was under Julius Busch, in drawing; then under Mr. Ropes, well remembered by the older citizens of Hartford; which, with

CHARLES DE WOLF BROWNELL.

the exception of many practical hints from Henry Bryant, was all he received before entering "Paul Potter's studio," and the "Academy of Leonardo da Vinci," up and down the Connecticut Valley. He also spent much time copying still-life with success. Thereafter for seven consecutive years he spent the winter in Cuba, making an extensive series of studies of the tropical scenery in oil, water-color, pencil, and pen-and-ink. In 1854 Trinity College, Hartford, conferred upon him the degree of A.M. In 1860 he moved his studio to New York, where he remained for five years. The next six years he passed in Europe with his wife and children. At present the artist resides in Bristol, R.I. Among his valuable works in Connecticut is the best painting ever made of the old

Charter Oak, now owned by Ex-Gov. Jewell; and a remarkable work
illustrative of Kingsley's lines, —

> "The sea-beast
> Stiffened, and stood brown rock in the wash of the wandering water," —

owned by Dr. Holmes.   A semicircular reef of rocks in a lonely bay,
with a few palms in the foreground, forms alone a fine picture; but, on

"THE CHARTER OAK." — BY CHARLES DE W. BROWNELL.

closer study, the reef of rocks assumes the outline of the sea-monster,
over which the surf is breaking.   In his knowledge of tropical scenery he
may be classed as having but few superiors.   One of his finest pictures is
an autumn-scene on the Connecticut River, ten miles above Saybrook.

CALVIN CURTIS.

The portrait-painter Calvin Curtis, at present located in Bridgeport,
was born in Stratford, Conn., July 5, 1822, a farmer's son.   Under his
mother's encouragement he procured books on drawing, and studied art by
himself, finally constructing for himself a palette and easel (the first he had
ever seen).   In December, 1841, he began study under Daniel Huntington,
spending his evenings at the Academy of Design.   In 1843 he opened a
studio of his own, and six years later returned to Connecticut, painting in
Birmingham and Waterbury till disabled by disease in 1856, which con-

fined him to his bed for nearly three years. In the fall of 1859, beginning to use his brush again, he went to Bridgeport, where he has since remained. His drawing is accurate, and he possesses remarkably good taste in coloring. Beside portraiture, he has of late, in a limited degree, extended his labors very successfully into the field of landscape. He is a man of strong will and superior education ; and those who are best able to judge, considering that every stroke of his brush for twenty years has been accompanied with a nervous pain, express warm commendation of his work especially as evidence of what might have been.

T. W. WOOD.

Thomas W. Wood is another of the celebrated artists to whose visits Connecticut owes much of the art-love that pervades her territory. He was born in Montpelier, Vt., Nov. 12, 1823 ; and came to Connecticut in 1857, painting in Winsted previous to an extended trip through Europe. He has lately developed, beside his achievements in oil-painting, a strength in water-color that promises to raise him even higher in the ranks of art.

THOMAS HICKS.

In 1866 Thomas Hicks honored the State with his presence while making copies in New Haven of Col. Trumbull's and Ralph Earl's portraits of Roger Sherman. Several copies in all were made for Mr. Moore of Trenton Falls, Secretary Evarts, and others. It would be impossible, within the limits of the subject, to offer to Mr. Hicks so much as a salutation from the State in accord with his position in art and society ; so that, attempting nothing more, the visit is simply recorded with reference to the influence that must be extended by the presence of such a visitor. He was born of Quaker parents in Newton, Penn., 1823 ; and in Mr. Tuckerman's book, so far as it extends, will be found an interesting and valuable account of his career.

J. DENISON CROCKER.

A landscape-painter of Norwich, J. D. Crocker, was born in Salem, Conn., Nov. 25, 1823. When nine years old, a wagon-maker, pleased with his mechanical bent, engaged him to work through his vacations at fifty cents a day. When twelve, this was given up to learn the trade of the silversmith, in which he became an expert. In 1840, while at work in a chair-manufactory, a portrait fell into his hands that had been sent there to be varnished. It was the first oil-painting he had ever seen, and filled him with a new desire. He stood before the glass, and painted himself. It induced him to become a portrait-painter. With the exception of a few hints from Charles Lanman, who was in Norwich at the time, and interested himself in his beginning, Mr. Crocker never received instruction in art, but gradually turned from portraiture to landscape, in which he has passed the greater part of his art-life. He is the author also of several valuable inventions, among them a cork-cutting machine in popular operation, and a file-machine ready for introduction.

NELSON AUGUSTUS MOORE.

N. A. Moore, an artist whose name is familiarly associated with Lake George, was born in Kensington, Conn., Aug. 2, 1824. His first impressions of art were gathered under peculiar circumstances, while holding a light for Milo Hotchkiss to paint the portrait of a child that had been killed by an accident, and upon which he was obliged to work through

"A SNOW-SCENE." — A STUDY IN OIL, BY N. A. MOORE.

the night. He obtained canvas, colors, and brushes, and at once began study by himself. When twenty-two he studied for one winter under Thomas S. Cummings, drawing from casts; and, later, portrait-painting under Daniel Huntington. In the spring of 1849 he began work in Kensington, but soon gave up portrait-painting almost entirely for landscape. Pastoral scenes have been made a specialty, and several snow-scenes possessing undeniable merit have gone from his studio. The foliage of the seasons on the various trees of New England has also been made a special study, with successful results. An ideal piece, "The Genius of Liberty," was received with much public favor. The artist's feeling for color is especially commendable.

HORACE C. JOHNSON.

H. C. Johnson of Waterbury, portrait-painter, was born in Oxford, Conn., in 1824. He had a strong love for art from childhood, but, being left an orphan very early in life, fell into the hands of those much opposed to a life devoted to the fine arts. He made many experiments with colors, and was an accomplished draughtsman before he received any instruction. In deference to the wishes of friends he first attempted a mercantile life, during which time he invented a valuable drill for artesian wells, the fame of which appeared even in Russia. Breaking away at last, he began a course of art-study under A. H. Emmons of Hartford, where he formed a life friendship with E. S. Bartholomew, with whom he entered the antique school of the National Academy, joining him again in Rome under his instructor Ferraro. He also studied in the English Life School, and returned to America to settle in Waterbury, where he has since practised the profession of the portrait-painter with a success that has left him no desire to change his location.

S. K. JONES.

A portrait-painter residing in New Haven, S. K. Jones, born in Clinton, Conn., February, 1825, at fifteen years of age formed the determination to undertake the profession of art. It was 1846, however, before an opportunity offered for study. This was under Alvin Fisher, who was then painting in New York. Without means to carry on the study, he was obliged to give it up in six months, and for several years painted as an itinerant. Since 1861 he has painted in New Haven, clinging throughout to portrait-painting, and attempting nothing else.

VINCENT COLYER.

The artist-member of the Connecticut legislature from Darien in 1877, Vincent Colyer, became a citizen of the State in 1866. He was born in Bloomingdale, now Central Park, New York, in 1825. His father

died of cholera in 1832, leaving a widow and seven children wholly unac-
customed to poverty.   To the following experiences Mr. Colyer attributes
the impulses which later in life caused him often to neglect his profession for benevolent and philanthropic labors.   After various positions as
errand-boy and clerk, he acted upon the advice of Edward Mooney, and
began the study of art under J. R. Smith, as well as several other
branches of study.   Drawing upon stone secured him work that paid his
expenses as he studied, including three years in the antique and life
schools in the National Academy.   During his study of anatomy he
worked for an entire summer, modelling every muscle of the human form,
and fitting it upon a skeleton.   In 1849 he was elected an associate of

VINCENT COLYER.

the National Academy.   His crayon-portraits brought him a hundred and
fifty dollars each; for the time, an exceedingly high figure.   Before the
Rebellion he was among the first to speak through a famous canvas,
"Freedom's Martyr," representing the burial of Barber by John Brown
and others; and shortly after, throwing every thing else one side, he
entered the army in various positions of Christian benevolence, chiefly
in connection with the New-York Young Men's Christian Association
(of which he was afterward president), the Brooklyn Association, and St.
George's Episcopal Church, originating among other good works the Christian Commission.   During the riots of 1863 Mr. Colyer also appeared
as the boldest of the friends of the colored man in New York; and

after the war, abandoning the position of curator of the Cooper Institute, he entered with as much spirit into a self-imposed labor with and for the Indians.

In 1866 he had bought a part of Contentment Island, a mile from Darien, and erected a studio there; and in 1872, after ten years of the above benevolence, Mr. Colyer left the Indian Commission in Washington, and retired to his studio and easel, having produced but one finished picture in the interim. He now began working up sketches he had made in the West during visits among the Indians.

In 1873 the yellow-fever, raging in the Mississippi Valley, extended a call, which Mr. Colyer gladly accepted, to enter the sanitary field again. At present he is once more devoting his time to art, having declined a second nomination to the State legislature which was unanimously offered him.

BENJAMIN AKERS.

Benjamin Akers, better known to the world and fame by his nickname "Paul," born in Saccarappa, Me., July, 1825, gained his first impressions of art while studying in Norwich in 1835, chiefly through the agency of a plaster cast in the house of Francis Finnegin, with whom he was living. His life is well known through other histories, resulting in the famed sculptor. He died in May, 1861.

RICHARD HINSDALE.

A son of the Mr. Hinsdale, long bookkeeper of the Hartford Bank, Richard by name, was born in Hartford in 1825. When twenty he attempted to take lessons of A. H. Emmons, but was restless and uneasy, unable to finish his first copy. Taking a French leave, he tried Mr. Hewins with the same result; then J. B. Flagg. After leaving Mr. Flagg, nothing was heard from him till he appeared again with a canvas under his arm, on which was a portrait, in black and white, of a shoe-dealer of the city, which he had executed from life, watching him through the window, then going home to work. The picture was a correct, forcible likeness. There was genius in it; but the genius was cruelly kept under a bushel throughout the artist's life by the same restless spirit that drove him about as a boy. He soon left Hartford, painted for a few months in Massachusetts, and then went to New York, where he deliberately laid down painting, and took up wood-engraving and the introduction of a "home gymnasium" which he had invented. In 1850 he returned to Hartford, and again planted his easel before him with much more determination than before. The result was at once evident. Dr. Beresford, Mr. Pond, and J. G. Batterson, were his chief patrons. Some excellent little landscapes and many ideal pieces of his painting still remain. He was very fond of children, and many times stopped in the street to play with them. Most of his ideal pictures evince the same fondness. The masterpiece of his short life in art was doubtless "The Haunted House," —a group of children in a dimly-lighted room, circled about a negress,

"GETTING A BITE." — RICHARD HINSDALE'S LAST PAINTING.

listening to ghost-stories. He left on his easel, when he died, "Getting a Bite," equal in execution to any thing he had done, — a youthful angler watching his cork go under. It is in possession of N. A. Moore of Kensington. He was altogether void of any executive ability beyond his art; always poor, and always careless of where the next meal was coming from till he became hungry. He died an early and very painful death, which cut short a life of very exceptional promise almost at the hour it began to assume shape and strength.

JOHN BUNYAN BRISTOL.

The father of the landscape-painter J. B. Bristol, whose work is so popular to-day, was a native of New Haven. This led the artist first to that city, and, later, up the Connecticut River and along the coast, on sketching trips. His "Evening on the Connecticut at Hartford" is a remarkably quiet, restful, and skilfully-executed work; which, indeed, are characteristics of all of Mr. Bristol's painting. He spent a summer sketching about the Four-Mile-Point Light below New Haven, and in the winter following produced three paintings from these sketches, and an admirable view of New Haven from the bay, that won critical admiration, especially for the atmospheric effects produced. Mr. Bristol was born in Hillsdale, a quiet town of New York (too quiet he found it before he had done with it), March 14, 1826. A single month's instruction under Henry Ary, a portrait-painter of Hudson, N.Y., formed his entire pupilage in art, beyond the constant study of the faithful artist; yet, in his peculiar line, Mr. Bristol has few superiors in the world of art. He was elected an academician in 1875, a time when it was so begrudgingly given as to make it a tribute of decided worth. He is also a member of the Artists' Fund and the Century Club. Connecticut, of course, lays no claim to the artist, but congratulates herself that he and his works are popular within her boundaries.

FREDERICK EDWIN CHURCH.

That task is most difficult, wisely and well to portray that which is great. To perform his task perfectly, the portrait-painter must for the time be one with his sitter, seeing and thinking as the sitter sees and thinks. Such is equally necessary for the biographer. But those men are few in one profession who are able to raise themselves to an understanding of the great men of another. In a history of art in Connecticut, biographies might be expected of several distinguished artists, including F. E. Church, to whom America owes much gratitude for the stimulus given to landscape-painting in this country, and the dignity accorded to American landscape-painting abroad. Owing to the conviction that such biographies would be impossible in the present case, they have not been attempted. The few facts following will give but a limited outline, that, so far as it extends, shall be accurate, closing with the comments of several journals of authority upon some of the artist's more important pieces.

Frederick Edwin Church was born on Temple Street, Hartford, Conn., in May, 1826. He was the only son of the late Joseph Church, a wealthy

and respected citizen, whose long life allowed him the pride and pleasure
of witnessing the artist's success in a life he had consented to his undertaking with many misgivings, counting art, of all professions, least wisely
undertaken on any uncertainty.   When sixteen, Mr. Church was received
as a private pupil in drawing by Benjamin H. Coe, and studied in color
under A. H. Emmons for six months.   Throughout his school-days, every
thing was made subservient to art ; and many reminiscences among his
friends are of fishing and pedestrian excursions, from which he returned
with his hat full of pencil-sketches of the clouds, — first studies of the sky
and atmosphere.   Once fairly entered upon art, his father was most zealous

"A TURKISH LANDSCAPE." — A STUDY IN OIL, BY F. E. CHURCH.

that he should receive every advantage.   Thomas Cole had never given
instruction ; but through the intervention of Daniel Wadsworth, an intimate friend of both, an arrangement was made whereby Mr. Church
became pupil and lifelong friend of the great landscape-painter.   The
early friendship that existed between Church, Bartholomew, and Ralph
Earl, proved mutually beneficial.   The characteristics of the man were
evident in the student, — resolution of purpose, tireless energy, and strict
honesty circling genius, aiding in the accomplishment of an unusual feat
in art, where prominence has been gained without application to the Old-
World art or to the old masters ; he never having been abroad until his
fame was as firmly established in Europe as America.   In the pursuit of

this knowledge he studied nature in every clime, from the heart of the tropics to the home of the icebergs. The genius developed among the wild ridges and stony reveries of the Catskills, the home of Cole, was marked throughout with strong individuality. He followed closely Cole's advice, — to make his brush his only walking-stick; and one of his first independent works, a view of West Rock, New Haven, at once obtained critical approval, and was purchased by Cyrus W. Field. The important result of his study in New England was an "Autumn Forest Scene," displayed at the academy, and purchased by his father. It was the first of the grand landscapes that have made his name famous. The sun is setting over a brilliant forest almost touched with fire. A cool lake, below the last rays of light, that are cut off by a distant mountain-top, reflects the warm picture. In the lake cattle are standing, enjoying their evening draught. The cloud-forms are characteristically rendered. The entire atmospheric effect is of New England, and no other place in the world. This picture prepared the way for the "Niagara." It was not that it was less skilfully wrought that it received less praise; but it surprised the critics and the public, and all waited expectantly. The "Niagara" came, and was as thoroughly Niagara. To the last rock, and cloud of spray, ray of sunlight, rainbow, and ripple, there was every thing pertaining to Niagara, nothing to any thing else. The world was satisfied, as following extracts will testify. Strictly speaking, the painting was the work of just six weeks, but, in reality, of a long and patient study and many sketches. The perfect accuracy in drawing was accomplished in a way solving to some degree the mystery of the success. The artist prepared two canvases of the same size. On one he experimented till his critical eye was satisfied with a line or an object; then placed it on the other. The result of his study was such an intimate knowledge of his subject, that long afterward he painted the main fall on a smaller canvas, in seven hours, from memory.

In 1853 Mr. Church sailed for South America, having long considered between the Rocky Mountains and the Andes. It was the third step in a career that has placed before the public so many of the distant wonders of the world and the glories of it. The hardships of such a trip into the wildest scenery of South America may not easily be portrayed in a limited space. Not satisfied with having been there once, Mr. Church repeated the undertaking in 1857 to assure himself that nothing of all the beauties should be forgotten. In the "Heart of the Andes," "Chimborazo," "Cotopaxi," "The Great Mountain Chain of New Granada," "Rainy Season in the Tropics," and many others, South America has been faithfully and minutely brought before us. The works are technically and practically different from any other productions of the artist, and of themselves create the impression that they must be true to leaf and flower, cloud and atmosphere, — true as the New England and the Niagara, with all the details of tropical flora, the tints of tropical atmosphere, the traits of tropical vegetation, combined with the majesty of the Andes, in marvellous harmony.

Then came a season among the icebergs, in which he was again discoverer, pioneer, conqueror. He spent the summer of 1859 along the coast of Labrador, accompanied by the Rev. Louis L. Noble, whose admirable book, " After Icebergs with a Painter," has rendered any thing further wholly unnecessary. " The Icebergs," in many respects, is the most remarkable picture which the artist has ever painted, and the finest work of the sort yet attempted. It was taken to England for exhibition, and purchased by Sir Edward Watkins.

In 1866 the artist turned his study to the Island of Jamaica. Mrs. Samuel Colt of Hartford owns the principal painting made from sketches on this trip. The artist's mother has also a fine view of the island. Last instead of first in the line, the Old World came to his assistance. His studies were chiefly of the scenery and ruins of Greece and Syria. " The Parthenon," an excellent specimen of drawing, he painted for Morris K. Jessup of New York; " Damascus from the Heights of Salchiyeh," for Walter Phelps of New York; " Syria by the Sea," for James F. Joy, Detroit; " The Valley of Santa Isabel," for John Buckingham, Chicago; " The Ægean Sea," for William H. Osborn, New York; the famous rock-temple of Arabia Petræa, for Mr. Phelps; an admirable view of Jerusalem, for T. M. Allyn of Hartford; " Morning on the Magdalena," for William E. Dodge, jun. His " Journey of the Pilgrim through the Wilderness," and " View of Quebec," now hang in the Wadsworth Gallery. The popularity of the works of Mr. Church has also given incentive to some of the greatest triumphs of the burin and chromo-lithograph.

The home of the artist near Rip Van Winkle's bed is essentially one of his works of art. It stands opposite Catskill, three miles south of the city of Hudson, on a hill six hundred feet above the river. The site is the result of a careful study of the river-banks, and commands so many views of varied beauty, that all the glories of the Hudson may be said to circle it. No better spot could have been found to keep fresh in mind an intimate knowledge of the clouds and atmosphere. The designs for the building were prepared by the artist, assisted by the architect Mr. Vaux.

The house, more properly castle, with its towers, reserved balconies, and pavilions, is thoroughly Persian, provincialized only where necessity demanded it. The walls, two and a half feet thick, are of rough stone

quarried on the spot, of a bluish tint, changing to a soft gray on the fracture. The cut work is of light brown and blue stone: the upper part of the principal tower is of red, yellow, and black brick, arranged in a unique pattern, giving the impression of mosaic-work. The main doorway is of light-brown stone, surrounded with mosaic tiles. The principal roofs are of red, green, and black slates, arranged in appropriate and elaborate patterns, relieved by a few gilt slates. The wooden cornices are painted in Persian colors, low and soft, with an effect of quiet harmony throughout. Instead of the Persian court, a large hall, cruciform, forms the centre of the building, from which open the various rooms. The art-gallery, with a ceiling eighteen feet high, is admirably lighted by four long windows on the north. The partitions are solid, and the whole is built on a foundation of the mountain-rock. The extensive grounds surrounding are in a constant state of arrangement under the direct supervision of the artist.

Here Mr. Church does the most of his work, though he also has a studio in New York. He has accomplished some feats of rapid execution, but generally paints slowly,—rarely over one large picture in a year, beside several smaller ones. Five hours of hard work before an easel, any artist will admit, is sufficient for a full day's work; but his indefatigable energy often holds him for ten hours upon a canvas. He paints standing, and with every minute progress inspects his picture from a distance. His gait, manner, and use of brush, all alike are indicative of the characteristic energy that has marked his life. In his painting he often walks between ten and fifteen miles a day.

He is radically a temperate man in all things, going for the purest impressions, profoundest truths, and most effective suggestions and inspiration, to the source of all in nature. Correspondingly there is little that can be considered imaginative in his work; yet the suggestions indicated in his touch are full of the imaginative element. His most signal success is in aerial perspective. As a colorist he is exact, adding incalculably to the real worth of his work. The local colors of New England never appear in the Catskills, nor the texture of the rocks and the characteristics of the Catskills' forests in any other landscape. The atmospheric condition to the quality, tone, and depth of cloud and sky formations, differ materially with locality. This distinction is one of the greatest victories of landscape-painting.

Mr. Church has been somewhat impeded in his work by a lameness in his right wrist; but the trouble has been greatly exaggerated by report. The world is in no danger of being deprived by it of the cunning of that right hand. But few of the vicissitudes of the young artist fell to his lot.

He began life, in a sense, a master.   When twenty-two he was elected an academician : and at the last meeting of the executive members (May, 1878) he was warmly urged to accept the vice-presidency preparatory to election to the presidency of the National Academy the coming year, when Mr. Huntington's term of office expires by limitation ; but he positively declined.

The following comments upon some of his more important works have been copied from the various journals as credited with name and date, speaking with authority as eye-witnesses and competent critics.

The New-York Albion, May, 1857, said, " Incontestably the finest oil-picture ever painted on this side of the Atlantic is now on exhibition on Broadway.   It is a view of the great Horseshoe Falls of Niagara.   We congratulate the artist on his brilliant success."

The London Times, Aug. 7, 1857, said, " Few scenes have been more often attempted by the pencil, and none have hitherto more completely laughed it to scorn.   But Mr. Church has painted this stupendous cataract with a quiet courage and a patient elaboration which leave us for the first time satisfied that even this awful reality is not beyond the range of human imitation."

The London Athenæum, July 18, 1857, said, " Mr. Church gives us with firmness and clear-sighted precision the tremendous level rush of the great line of water, as calmly, and with terrible calmness, it moves towards its grave in the great hell-pool from whence the rainbow springs with its celestial arch."

The Liverpool Mercury, July 16, 1858 : " Apart from accuracy in any minor objects, the excellency of the painting is the artist's wonderful conception and portrayal of the mighty waters in their everlasting turbulence, and the fantastic play and dazzle of light upon them.   Alike inimitable and unparalleled are the rainbow, the rose-colored cloud, and distant horizon."

Of " The Heart of the Andes," the New-York Evening Post, April 30, 1859, says, " In choice of subject, harmony of color, management of detail, &c., it possesses every themical merit ; while in poetry, and grandeur of sentiment, we can imagine nothing superior."

Harper's Weekly, May 7, 1859 : " In the manipulation of this picture Mr. Church seems to have bridged the gulf between the exactitude of the Pre-Raphaelites and the breadth of the Post-Raphaelites. The foreground is elaborated with a patient care, a thoughtful detail, and a loyalty to nature, that Millais might envy ; while the whole scene has a vastness, a calmness, and quiet breadth, which Salvator never attained."

A STUDY FROM THE SANTA ISABEL VALLEY, BY F. E. CHURCH.

T. Buchanan Read, speaking of the picture, wrote to the New-York Evening Post, May 7, 1859, —

> "Here blooms a world that fears nor cold nor drouth,
> The lavish luxury of the teeming South,
> The carnival of summer far and near,
> In lands where summer lords it all the year;
> And over all, his Andean front aglow,
> Great Chimborazo sits his throne of snow."

The Christian Intelligencer, June 2, 1859: "'The Heart of the Andes' is a complete condensation of South America into a single focus of magnificence."

When on exhibition in New York, the receipts at the door in a single day amounted to $538; and during the month, $3,172.

The London Daily News, July 4, 1859: "The Pre-Raphaelite minuteness and self-evident accuracy of the foreground, and the broadly generalized, delicately graduated, and atmospheric distance of this picture, prove that the artist unites almost a contrariety of gifts. The breadth and finish are almost perfectly harmonized."

The London Morning Post, July 7, 1859: "It bespeaks not only the painter's skill of hand, but the poet's sympathetic appreciation of the spirit and sentiment of scene; and it conveys to the spectator at a single glance a more faithful idea of the romantic charm of mountain solitudes than could be derived from the perusal of whole chapters of written description."

The London Literary Gazette, July 7, 1859, says, "The feeling will be one of surprise at the artist-like knowledge and themical mastery which the picture almost everywhere displays."

The Art Journal, October, 1859, says, "Here is obviously one of those mental mirrors of a rare brightness which have literally the power to fix and transfer their affections; manifestly a gaze of extraordinary clearness and vigilance, a gifted hand swift to follow it with graceful strength and likeness, a tender and capacious spirit which unites harmoniously the minute and the vast, the delicate and the forcible, the defiant and the mysterious, and can reduce multitude and diversity to simplicity and order under the sweet sovereignty of beauty."

The New-York Herald, Dec. 5, 1859, says, "From the exhibition of Church's great picture, 'The Heart of the Andes,' may be dated the inauguration of a new art-epoch. That extraordinary picture may be said to embody all the peculiarities and excellences which have given the stamp of originality to American art."

Of "The Icebergs," the New-York Tribune, April 24, 1861, says,

" It is an absolutely wonderful picture, — a work of genius that illustrates the time and the country producing it. Its idea is grand, and the artist hand that has put it upon canvas is worthy of the artist mind that conceived it."

This picture was first exhibited in New York at the outbreak of the war, and with true loyalty the proceeds were contributed to the " patriot fund " just forming.

The London Morning Star, June 22, 1863 : " We can believe that a truer picture was never painted."

The London Post : " Church is a delicate and accurate draughtsman, a patient student of Nature under her most difficult and perplexing aspects, a pure and brilliant colorist, and a master of that supreme art of composition which can never be taught, and never be acquired."

"The Heart of the Andes " is at present owned by David Dows of New York, who bought it privately before the auction-sale of a collection containing it. The " Niagara " was bought by the Corcoran Gallery, for twelve thousand five hundred dollars, in the auction-sale of the John Taylor Johnson collection. This, considering price and purchaser, was the rarest compliment that could have been paid to the artist and his work. "The Parthenon," painted for Morris K. Jessup, and " Morning in the Tropics," a large, exquisite, and grand scene, owned by William E. Dodge, jun., have gone to Paris for the present exposition. "Jerusalem," " Jamaica," " The New-England Autumn," " The Pilgrim in the Wilderness," beside many smaller views, are owned in Hartford. " The Ægean Sea," another picture that is highly praised by those who have seen it, is owned by W. H. Osborn, New York.

Mr. Church is as actively and enthusiastically engaged in art to-day as ever in his life. He occasionally paints a little in New York, but generally at his home, being one of the few, whether in art or other professions, who, being all in all within themselves, are able to sever themselves from the busy whirl of life, from which one borrows life. May it be long before that right hand is still, and the world presented with its last picture from Connecticut's gifted son !

WALES HOTCHKISS.

Wales Hotchkiss, born in Bethany, Conn., 1826, studied portrait-painting first under George W. Flagg in New Haven, and in 1843 went with him to New York. As a boy, a passion for drawing heads had led him, among other adventures, to arrange all of the dignitaries of the church on the margins of the hymn-books. His first work in oil was an experiment in house-paint, with his brother for model. The success was so great, that his parents reluctantly yielded to his ambition to become a portrait-painter. A serious accident while yachting so much impaired his health, that his work in art has been at times materially hindered. After completing his study, he returned to New Haven. His forte is in

WALES HOTCHKISS.

water-color. He has also painted portraits and historical pieces in oil, that have been criticised as possessing force, energy, a good eye for color, and originality. Nine years ago the artist moved to Northampton, where he still resides.

CHARLES HINE.

An intimate friend of Wales Hotchkiss, Charles Hine, born in the same town (Bethany), and a year later (1827), was brought while a boy to New Haven. When fifteen he began his study of art, first under George W. Flagg; then in Hartford, under his brother Jared B. Flagg. He painted for two years in Derby, returning in 1846 to New Haven for ten years, during which time he was fully occupied on head and figure pieces, and found his work eagerly sought after. In 1857 he moved to New York. His masterpiece was a nude figure entitled "Sleep," the result of two years of labor, and commented upon by critics as the finest work of the kind ever attempted in America. He inherited consumption from his mother, and very early in his career it began its inroads. At last, unable to work longer in his studio, he returned to New Haven, and for some time painted fancy pieces while lying on his back. N. D. Sperry of New Haven has the last work of the artist, "A String of Pearls," a charming little boudoir-scene, in which the lace and silk costume of a finely-drawn female figure, as well as the string of pearls she is arranging about her neck, are admirably painted. Mr. Hine died July 29, 1871, having left the possibilities of his life evidently far from realized, but having made much of each opportunity as it was offered him.

ADALBERT WUNDER.

In 1855 a German artist named Adalbert Wunder set up his easel in Hartford, remaining until 1869. He was born in Berlin Feb. 5, 1827. When sixteen he began a three-years' course of study in the Royal Academy of Design, and private instruction under Professor Herbig, and for two years thereafter in the Dresden Academy. He painted some portraits in oil; but crayon and India-ink heads were his specialties, in which he gained an important local reputation. He worked with great rapidity and much skill. One of his finest pieces was a pastel head of Mr. Bryant, which was unfortunately destroyed by some of that artist's pupils, who, overcome by a sudden desire to make a neat, orderly room of his studio during his absence, carefully dusted the pastel head among other things. Mr. Wunder was a public-spirited man, ready to engage in any undertaking that might promote a sympathy for art. He is now painting in Hamilton, Ontario.

GEORGE F. BOTTUME.

A portrait-painter well known in the eastern part of the State, George F. Bottume, was born in Baltic, Conn., July, 1828. It was a common acceptation among the "country-folk," that George Bottume was "cut out" for a painter; and at thirteen he went to New York to study. The first three years he was obliged to spend under Albertson, a sign-painter born in Norwich in 1808, where he died March 27, 1846. Bottume then studied for a year under Solomon Fanning, and opened a studio in Norwich. At the end of two years, there being already several portrait-painters in Norwich, he left the city, and has since continued portrait-painting in many localities, arriving at last in Springfield, Mass., where he still resides. His work is chiefly portraiture, though he has also produced some landscapes. His colors are warm, his style easy, his likenesses in portraits good. He paints rapidly, having nearly completed

"ON THE FARMINGTON RIVER," RY JAMES M. HART.

some of his best pictures in a single day; which of itself, probably, has a tendency to make an artist less careful for his reputation and his purse.

GEORGE F. WRIGHT.

Among the leading men in portraiture, emanating from Connecticut, is George F. Wright, born in Washington, Conn., Dec. 19, 1828. As a lad he was placed in preparation for a classical education under the Rev. Isaac Jones of Litchfield. He entered a studio when a boy, with an attempt at painting for a criticism. "Are you an artist?" inquired the painter. "No, sir; but I am going to be," was the prophetic reply. He settled first in Wallingford, and in May, 1847, succeeded Mr. Bartholomew as custodian of the Wadsworth Athenæum Gallery. The following year he studied in the life-school at the National Academy, and, returning to Hartford, painted portraits very acceptably for five years; after which he spent two years abroad, — in Germany under Professor Graeflei, court-painter of Baden, and a summer in Rome. Returning, he has painted in many Southern and Western cities, but principally in Hartford. He painted many of the governors of Illinois, and many of Connecticut. His work is remarkable for its power, its natural flesh-tints, its accuracy of likeness. Portraits of T. K. Brace and the last Gov. Trumbull are among his best work. Charles L. Elliott remarked at an academy exhibition, pointing to one of Mr. Wright's heads, "I have much cause to fear that man." Few men have possessed the genius, and given the promise, of George F. Wright; but his life has been one of varied experiences, in which, while he has done much masterly work, he has apparently failed to recognize his own talent.

JAMES M. HART.

By very good fortune to the State, and (may it not be taken *amiss*) by very good fortune to the artist too, James M. Hart, the popular landscape and rising cattle painter of America, was tempted, thirteen years ago, under the solicitation of President Porter and others, to test the beautiful mysteries of the Connecticut Valley about Farmington, first in 1865, and again two years later. One of the results has been some of the finest specimens of the artist's work; another was the accomplishment of a life-partnership with a lady who was at the time sketching in the Farmington Valley. A view of the river near Farmington was contributed by Mr. Hart to the Paris Exposition of 1867. The London Athenæum critic, after speaking of the works of Cropsey, Bierstadt, and others, wrote of this picture, "Better in painting and finer in sentiment than these is Mr. James M. Hart's 'River Tunxis in Connecticut,'" &c. His famous picture, "Peaceful Homes," and several later works of great popularity, also hail from Farmington and thereabout.

The artist was born in Kilmarnock, Scotland, in 1828. His first taste of art came with the proverbially art-suggestive drudgery of the carriage-shop. After studying for a year under Schirmer in Düsseldorf, he established himself in Albany, N.Y.; five years later moving to New-York City, where he has since remained, enjoying very high popularity. He was made an academician in 1859, and is one of the most enthusiastic laborers for the advancement of art to be found in the country. While Connecticut can lay no claim upon him, she is certainly entitled to share in congratulation upon his brilliant career.

ALBERT F. BELLOWS.

Another instance with the preceding is that of Albert F. Bellows, born in Milford, Mass., 1829. Though an artist from the cradle, his father endeavored to strike a bargain with imperious Nature by securing

ALBERT F. BELLOWS.

him a position as pupil under A. B. Young, the distinguished architect of Boston. But, in spite of architecture, he was bound to be a painter. After three years of this pupilage when twenty years old, he graduated,

"THE DROVE AT THE FORD," BY J. M. HART,
OWNED BY THE CORCORAN GALLERY.

and formed a partnership with J. D. Toule, an established architect, to do the artistic designing, while Mr. Toule attended to the construction. Success was not wanting; but satisfaction was. At the end of his first year he gave up resistance, and surrendered himself to the prompting of his love of painting, and soon became principal of the New-England School of Design. When twenty-seven he resigned the position, and, after a careful study of art in the first Paris Exposition, became a pupil in the Royal Academy of Art in Antwerp, of which he was afterward made an honorary member. He established himself in New York as portrait and figure painter, and in 1857 was made an academician. He gradually withdrew partially from figure-painting in favor of landscapes; but a

"A CONNECTICUT HOMESTEAD." — THE REVOLUTIONARY ELMS OF EAST HARTFORD, BY A. F. BELLOWS.

popular characteristic of his work has become his combination of figure-life with landscape. On the revival of water-color painting in America Mr. Bellows was found among the first, and has become one of its most powerful supporters. At present his studies are all made in water-color. The artist's principal work in Connecticut, and in some respects the principal work of his life thus far, is a series prepared and completed in Windsor — "Life's Day, or Three Times across the River" — in 1860. The pictures, three in number, represent the same scene — the river opposite Windsor — in spring, summer, and winter. In the first, parents are rowing a baby across the river to the village church for baptism. In the second the bride stands in the boat, and the spire rises above the branches on the opposite shore. In the last the river is frozen; the trees are loaded with snow: the moon, just rising, lights the path across the ice for a slowly-moving funeral-procession, and touches the church-spire with light as if it were a beacon to signal the way to God's Acre. Every figure of the various groups is modelled from life.

Edwin Forrest bought these pictures; and, in the bestowal of his estate, they went to the Forrest Home for Actors. Engravings of the three are owned by many in Windsor, Hartford, and elsewhere.

Since that time nearly all of Mr. Bellows's important sketching trips in America have been in Connecticut. A characteristic choice is from the old towns and villages, old streets, and old houses, of old-time New England. Among his latest and best works in water-color is the old East-Hartford Street, including the centenarian gable-roofed homestead and the Revolutionary elms. This piece is one of two by Mr. Bellows exhibited in the present Paris Exposition.

WILLIAM RODERICK LAWRENCE.

A young man of peculiarly interesting artistic ability, very little exerted, however, in a professional way, W. R. Lawrence, was born March 3, 1829; and died of inherited consumption, Oct. 9, 1856. He spent his entire life in Hartford, except during a few months of study in New York. When only four years old, motives of art were demonstrated in the skill with which he drew an elephant which was passing the window with a menagerie. In accordance with his father's wishes, he obtained a medical education, though he never practised the profession. He was a devoted student of natural history, and it was from drawing and coloring bugs and insects that he finally found for himself a place in art. He was very near-sighted, which accounts for the lack of color-effect in his pictures; otherwise there is much that is artistic about them. During the winters of 1848 and 1849 he studied in the National Academy. He was also a poet of fine feeling and elegant expression, and much before his age in an extravagant delight in collecting ancient pottery. He was for some time secretary of the Natural-History Society, of which the well-known Deacon Turner was president. His most important work was the complete illustration of a large medical treatise on the circulation of the blood. He also illustrated Mrs. Sigourney's "Poems of the Sea." After his death Mrs. Sigourney wrote a beautiful memorial poem, which was extensively published, appearing first in "The New-York Ledger" Oct. 11, 1856. His paintings were all of a peculiarly imaginative tendency, carefully drawn. There are two of them in the Wadsworth Gallery, — "The Royal Children," and "Napoleon at Waterloo." He was extremely fond of children, often using them as models for his work. His life was a smooth current, his death a quiet close.

JOB B. SPENCER.

A painter of fruits, flowers, and animals, Job B. Spencer, born in Salisbury, Conn., 1829, was educated a house-painter. After accumulating a reserve-fund, and in a few rough sketches testing the probability of his accomplishing feats in higher art, he went to New York and studied for two years; then settled in Scranton, Penn., where his reputation stands well among local artists. Several of his pictures are owned in Salisbury. He is a somewhat eccentric man, with a keen sense of the ridiculous.

BENJAMIN F. ELLIOTT.

The landscape and portrait painter of Middletown, B. F. Elliott, was born in that city Sept. 26, 1829; and died there Sept. 6, 1870. His opportunities were limited for gaining instruction; but in 1860 he opened a studio, producing work that disclosed a conscientious, painstaking artist. He worked for a year upon portraits for Kellogg Brothers in Hartford. He was quiet, reserved, and utterly unable to thrust his own work forward in a way that would bring it before the public.

WILLIAM OLIVER STONE.

The well-known portrait-painter, William O. Stone, was born in Derby, Conn., in 1830. Very early in life he determined to become a painter. For this resolve ample promise gave the best authority, and following success was an unqualified verdict. As is too often the case, many hard battles were fought before, at the age of eighteen, he was allowed to place himself under Nathaniel Jocelyn of New Haven to study art. He lost all of his previous studies and work in the fire which destroyed Mr. Jocelyn's studio in 1849, and in 1851 moved to New York virtually to begin life.

Here he rose very rapidly both as an artist, and in the estimation of many friends; for, though he never married, Mr. Stone was always popular in a very large circle. As a critic his opinion stood high in New York. Perhaps he was too popular, and too fond of society, to fulfil the vast possibilities that lay before his youth: certainly he had not developed all of his power when he died (at Newport, R.I., Sept. 15, 1875), though no one would deny him a place among the first artists of America. In 1859 he became an academician of the National Academy, and in 1863 was elected a member of the Century Club; in both of which he filled important offices, and was thoroughly respected. He was remarkably kind-hearted, and his

WILLIAM OLIVER STONE.

gentleness and sweetness of character were imparted to all his work. He followed portraiture throughout his life, achieving especial success in female heads and children's portraits.

HENRY A. LOOP.

The distinguished portrait and figure painter H. A. Loop, besides passing several summers in New Haven, and many in Lakeville, Litchfield County, Conn., has connected his name with Connecticut's art, in being the instructor, and becoming the husband, of the pride of the State among female artists, — Miss Harrison of New Haven. Very much might justly be said of Mr. Loop; but yielding the pleasure to the necessity of brevity in all these sketches, chiefly those not of native Connecticut artists, simply the outline of the life that has led him to his present success will be inserted. He was born in Hillsdale, Columbia County, N.Y., in 1831, and in 1841 went to Great Barrington, Mass., to school. At the age of sixteen he entered a clerkship there, and for three years endeavored to fight against the ambition to appear in the field of art. When nineteen he entered the studio of Henry Peters Gray, where he remained a year, and, after some preliminary practice in painting portraits and landscapes, opened

"AENONE." AN ACADEMY PAINTING. BY HENRY A. LOOP.

a studio in New York. Six years later he sailed for Paris, and entered the atelier of Couture. There he studied a year, and spent another year in Florence and Rome, studying from life, and painting a few original pictures. After returning to America he resumed portrait-painting, relieving the monotony with an occasional original figure-piece. In 1867 with his wife and daughter he again crossed the ocean, visiting Paris, Rome, Perugia, and Venice, and remaining abroad two years. During this time he painted but one portrait, — that of Judge Skinner of Buffalo, — but produced several fine original works, and made several excellent copies. Thus educated, he has been prepared to exert a favorable influence for art wherever he should choose his field of labor; and it is fortunate for Connecticut that the choice for summer-work has been that State.

Mr. Loop's work is characteristic for warmth of color, broad and simple treatment, and great refinement and delicacy, especially in the representation of the nude figures which he has lately undertaken with a success unrivalled in America. As a draughtsman he stands very high : his conceptions and general designs are exceptionally fine. In 1861 he was made an academician, and in 1863 elected a member of the Century Club.

W. R. WHEELER.

The portrait-painter W. R. Wheeler, for seventeen years established in Hartford, was born in Michigan (Scio, Washington County), 1832, whither his father had gone from Middletown, Conn., his native place, in 1830. Art had been a strong incentive evident in the life of his aunt Lydia W. Pierson, and also in the life of his father. To encouragement, instead of rebuke, Mr. Wheeler owes much of his early success. His first lessons were received from an itinerant miniature-portrait painter ; and at the age of fifteen he entered the field, working at very low prices, boarding where he painted, and saving every thing, till three years later he was able to study in Detroit for a year under Professor Bradish, art-teacher in the Detroit University. In 1855 Mr. Wheeler was married, and moved to Hartford. His success has held him in that city, without change. His peculiar forte is with children's faces, of which he has probably painted more than any other artist who ever worked in the city. His heads are well modelled, good likenesses, and pleasing in color.

Though portrait-painting has been a branch to which he has devoted his life, he has within a few years made some very successful experiments in landscape-studies.

A. D. SHATTUCK.

Ten years ago (in 1868) one of the most careful of American pastoral-painters came with his family to Granby, Conn., and two years afterward bought himself a farm of twenty-eight acres there, where he keeps much of the excellent stock that from time to time appears in his pictures. He was born in Francestown, N.H., March 6, 1832, and educated in art under Alexander Ransom and at the National Academy, of which he was made an academician in 1861.

Many of his best pieces are from studies made about his farm and

"A STUDY OF SHEEP."—BY A. D. SHATTUCK.

through the State. A large landscape by him, "Sunday Morning in New England," has gained almost unqualified praise. The work is emphatically well executed, fitly and naturally expressing the subject. It is direct, simple, and truthful, without attempt to surprise by novel effects, or feats of elaborate realism. The pleasure it gives the beholder is through its simplicity, and fidelity to nature,—a pleasure which is sure to be enduring.

The artist is a faithful student of his art, and at present makes a specialty of sheep and cows, where he excels many, and is excelled by few. He is a thorough, affable gentleman, and may well be considered a valuable acquisition to Connecticut. Mr. Tuckerman gives an elaborate sketch.

TRUMAN HOWE BARTLETT.

T. H. Bartlett, born in the town of Dorset, Bennington County, Vt., in 1836, to all intents upon a marble-quarry, when nineteen learned the trade of a stone-cutter, and is now located in Paris. He has received orders from several sources in Connecticut for monumental work and some bronze pieces. He worked in Waterbury in 1862, in New Haven in 1863 and after, leaving America in 1867. In Waterbury the Benedict monument, in Hartford the statue of Dr. Wells, are among his works.

JOHN L. FITCH.

The forest-painter, John L. Fitch, was born in Hartford in 1836. He began the study of art under Julius Busch, and later studied under George F. Wright in Hartford, preparatory to sailing for Europe in 1855, where for three years he studied drawing in Munich, and painting for one year in Milan under the three Zimmermanns, — Professor Albert, Richard, and Max. He painted in Hartford from 1859 to 1866. Immediately on his return his work followed closely after his masters, which was not a style popular in America; but gradually he has dropped the objectionable features of the Zimmermanns, retaining their excellences with great refinement in detail, and depth of feeling, which render his studies of the gnarled forest-trees, the rocks and wild ravines, exceedingly interesting and artistic. In 1866 he moved to New York, and has since remained there, with the exception of a short trip to Germany in 1871. In 1867 he was elected a member of the Century Club, and now (in 1878) for the fifth time holds the position of chairman of the Art Committee. In the fall of 1877 the artist distinguished himself in a new direction by saving the valuable collection of art in the rooms of the Century Club from destruction by fire, through characteristic energy that called forth a graceful vote of thanks. Mr. Fitch is also an associate of the National Academy, and a member of the Artists' Fund Society. He is a man of very refined tastes in art, and within a few years his work has rapidly improved toward the making of a masterly picture from his exceedingly fine studies. His field is somewhat limited, except as he has several times very successfully attempted the introduction of water-scenes; one of the finest pieces of his painting being " Twilight on John's Brook," an admirable, quiet evening view, well hung in the fifty-third annual exhibition of the National Academy. There is certainly that spirit in all of his work which must retain for him a lasting name in art. Mrs. Samuel Colt of Hartford has one of his finer pieces in her gallery.

CHARLES AKERS.

Charles Akers, born in Maine Oct. 15, 1836, the sculptor and crayon artist, at present established in New York, in 1860, 1869, and 1875 occupied a studio in Waterbury, Conn., making crayon heads and marble busts which were both artistic and popular. He is an artist of much merit, and an elegant writer.

OTTO KESSLER.

A German artist named Otto Kessler gained considerable celebrity in Connecticut from 1863 to 1865. He was born in Berlin in 1837, and was a pupil of Wilhelm Köhner, whom he subsequently followed to Hartford. His wife, an American lady of unusual dignity, persuaded him to seek another field in October, 1865. He painted rapidly, often finishing a life-size bust in oil in a single day. He worked largely through the Jewish population, and received good prices. But Otto Kessler loved the wine-glass better than his wife or art, and neither was able to hold him in restraint. He has now returned to Berlin, where his mother is still living.

GEORGE EDWARD CANDEE.

G. E. Candee, a resident artist of New Haven, was born there Dec. 24, 1838. He met with much opposition to his desire to study art, but was at last allowed to hire himself to an ornamental painter. This was followed by a few lessons from Joseph Kyle, a portrait-painter. This, with about as many lessons in water-color, constituted his entire instruction. His first independent endeavor in art was as a water-colorist; but the lack of popularity of water-color work induced him to connect with it portrait-painting, while by himself he proceeded to study both. This course he changed in time, giving his chief attention to fruit and flower pieces. In 1865 he moved to New York, remaining a year, and in 1870 sailed for Europe, spending a winter in Rome, and summer in Perugia. Most of his work is owned in New Haven, including several foreign landscapes in water-color and oil, and some very acceptable figure-pieces.

R. M. SHURTLEFF.

From 1869 to 1875 R. M. Shurtleff occupied a studio in Hartford. He was born in Rindge, N.H., 1838; and, before he was able to read, his pictures were the pride of the family. Later, however, he found much objection to his becoming an artist, and when twenty-one had not seen a picture of any merit. In 1859 he began drawing on wood for engravers, studying evenings in the Lowell Institute, and designing for several illustrated magazines. In 1861 he joined the New-York Ninty-ninth Regiment, with which he was the first Northern officer wounded and captured in an engagement. In 1869 he came to Hartford and began designing for the American Publishing Company, at the same time taking up work in color. He is strictly a landscape-painter, but characteristically introduces animal-life with marked ability, catching motion with particular success. He is also rapidly becoming a strong water-color painter. During his stay in Hartford he was actively connected with the Hartford Art Association.

HARRY IVES THOMPSON.

H. I. Thompson, at present successfully established in New Haven as portrait and figure painter, was born in West Haven Jan. 31, 1840.

" LIBRARY-SCENE." — A STUDY BY H. I. THOMPSON.

When twenty years of age he was conducting a grocery-store in his native place, devoting his leisure time to painting still-life pieces from subjects about him. In 1861 his store was abandoned for art, and he entered the drawing-school of Benjamin H. Coe, which three years later he conducted, Mr. Coe retiring. This position he held till 1867. Mr. Thompson is young, and enthusiastic in his profession; and, while he has done much that entitles him to a position in Connecticut art, he has apparently the will and ability to do much more. He painted the portrait of Gen. Putnam that hung in the Connecticut Cottage at the Philadelphia Centennial Exhibition. In the fifty-second annual exhibition at the National Academy he presented a large portrait of Dr. Leonard Bacon of Yale, which is thus far his best work in portraiture. It is natural, lifelike, and boldly painted. Another excellent work is a portrait of Judge E. K. Foster, hanging in the Superior-Court room at New Haven. He has made a decided progress in the past three years.

WILLIAM GEDNEY BUNCE.

A son of James M. Bunce of Hartford, William Gedney Bunce, now a resident artist of Paris, was born in Hartford in 1840. His first impressions of childhood were a love of art. This feeling, being overpowered by parental objection, was virtually set aside.

When sixteen years old, driven by a restless spirit waiting development, he studied drawing under the direction of Julius Busch.

In 1863 Mr. Bunce went to New York, and began a course of instruction in oil-painting under William Hart. Decided success and rapid progress induced him to accompany Mr. Hart, the following summer, upon a sketching-trip through Maine. As a boy and youth, he had been in every thing an enthusiast; and, once his heart being fixed upon painting, he threw the whole enthusiasm of his life into it. Several unfortunate financial investments acted to seal the fate that would place him permanently in the ranks of art. In 1867 he sailed for Europe, going at once to Paris. Here he began again the study of drawing, realizing that there was his principal deficiency. Later he left for Munich, where he studied for a year; then walked through Switzerland with DuBois, and established himself in Rome, remaining there for six years, and making excursions over Italy.

He has spent the past four winters in Paris, the summers in Venice, and is a thorough admirer of French art. He writes, "I stay in Paris because I think I can learn more here than anywhere else in the world. I have lived as an artist in America, England, Germany, Italy, and Holland, and consider that France takes the lead. I think the Paris *salon* the best and hardest place to work for in the world. I want to live in my native land,

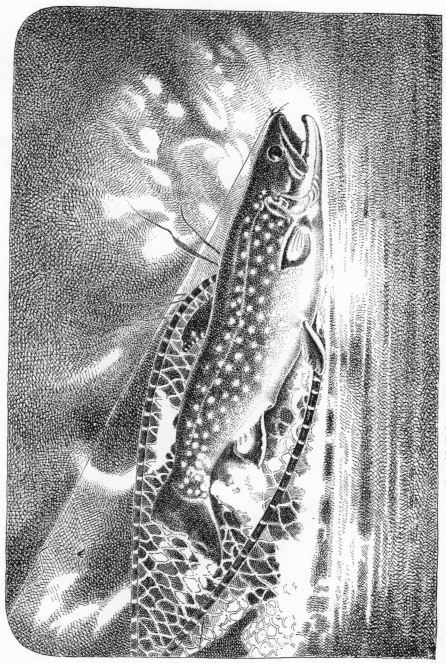

"A CRITICAL MOMENT," BY GURDON TRUMBULL.

and I hope I yet may; but older countries, like older men, can teach me the most as yet." His pictures have lately been entirely Venetian views. His style since leaving America has naturally changed materially. Many of his pictures are owned in Hartford. They are bold and free in painting, and of strong, rich color and warm tints, well adapted to his choice of views. His forte is as a colorist. His scenes are weird and often melancholy spots, selected where the power of color may be most effective and undisturbed. A Venetian landscape of his was hung on the line in the Paris *salon* for March, 1877; and the same in the first New-Society Exhibition in New York.

An over-critical spirit regarding his own work has been to his disadvantage at times. He is slow to speak, but, when aroused upon a point of interest, a fine conversationalist.

EUGENE BENSON,

A singularly brilliant man in mind and talent, spent four years in New Haven, leaving an impression upon the art-life of the city and state that will not soon be forgotten. He was born at Hyde Park on the Hudson Nov. 1, 1840.

As a boy he had been taught by necessity the value of economy. While a student, and during the first three years of his life as an artist, he struggled against a poverty that would have baffled many an aspirant. He lived in New York, practising forced denials that could hardly be credited if repeated. He increased a very small income by contributing upon the lowest terms to several of the New-York dailies. Unfortunately for art, the support thus received as a friend in need lured him from the work for which he was sacrificing every thing. He possessed evident talent as a writer; and from writing of necessity he was soon, almost unconsciously, writing as a luxury at the expense of his pictures. Poverty sharpens the senses, and creates almost an insane fondness for that which affords relief. His literary work rapidly increased in excellence. From time to time able art-criticisms appeared in " The New-York Evening Post " over the signature " Proteus." The authorship was fastened upon the obscure artist. From that time Eugene Benson became one of the finest art-critics who ever wrote in America. In 1869 Mr. Benson left New York, and moved to New Haven. He resided near East Rock. During his life in New Haven, his attention was about equally divided between writing and painting. In both his merits must be freely acknowledged, though the public bestowed greater honor upon the writer than the painter.

In 1873 Mr. Benson went abroad, and, with no material exceptions, has since resided there. Mrs. Benson is a daughter of Dr. Milan of Geneva. Her daughter is the graceful and talented author of " Kismet."

Mr. Benson's work is confined to figure-painting and portraits. He excels in modelling the figure in various attitudes, and has the reputation of great frankness, and fidelity to fact, in his representation of foreign dress, costume, and peculiarities. In portraits he is equally successful in obtaining a good likeness. Professor Weir of New Haven has in his possession two portraits of Miss Julia Fletcher, which are indicative of a free, bold touch, and an effective use of colors. His work possesses the same delicacy and the same motive of poetry that is so finely expressed in his æsthetic criticisms. He was elected to the Artists' Fund in 1861, but fell back through neglect.

GURDON TRUMBULL.

The finest fish-painter of America, Gurdon Trumbull, was born in Stonington, Conn., May 5, 1841. In 1852 he came to Hartford. His first and most lasting associations were with artists, and almost insensibly the whole tenor of his life was turned in that direction. His first work in oil was upon landscapes, though his earlier drawings had been of fish. He studied for a time under F. S. Jewett; then went to New York, and became a pupil of James M. Hart. His progress as a student was not that of ordinary plodding, but bore promise of genius. Unfortunately for the art, Mr. Trumbull's circumstances have been such that he has never been urged beyond the dictates of his fancy to follow a profession. Few of his pictures have come before the public: indeed, he has painted but very little.

In landscape his masterpiece is "A Moorish Watch-Tower on the Coast of Spain," in possession of William C. Prime, LL.D., which was copied in chromo in France shortly after its appearance. From landscape he undertook flower-painting, feeling that he had not touched the responding note in his nature with exactness. Some of these flower-pieces were exceptionally fine, but not satisfactory to the artist. At last he found, in the painting of fish, the branch of art in which he was destined to lead. His pictures are noticeably remarkable as portraits. They are not dead, rigid outlines, hung upon a wall or lying on a table, nor the lazily floundering fish that may be seen through a glass at an aquarium. They are on fire with life; they are vigorous to every fin. He has chosen his scenes where activity is the soul of the subject; such views as only the sportsman gains and can appreciate. There is nothing morbid or monotonous in them. They are microscopically perfect, each scale, eye, fin, tissue about the gills,

G. Trumbull.

being a study in itself, yet so skilfully executed that distance lends enchantment, and completes the figure with the excitement of motion and vitality.
Foremost among his productions is " A Critical Moment," exhibited in the
Centennial Art Gallery at Philadelphia.   A leading metropolitan journal
commented upon it, " The naturalist can make as good a study from this,
so far as externals go, as he could from the fish itself.   It is a delicious
work to look at, and may safely be ranked, with Mr. Trumbull's other
pictures of this class, the finest fish-paintings that have been seen in any
times."   The trout has taken the hook, and made a last mad rush, which
has proved successful.   The tackle has broken, and he is going over the

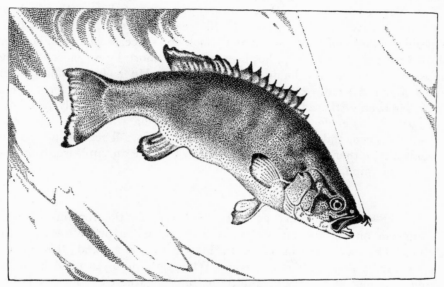

" STUDY OF A BLACK BASS." — BY G. TRUMBULL.

falls with mouth open, in an almost exhausted plunge for liberty, his brilliant sides flashing in the green-and-white spray that covers him.   The
work shows most astonishing care ; the gossamer fins absolutely undulate ;
and, as one watches, he almost expects to see the trout disappear from the
green flood, leaving it, flecked with its white foam, alone in the frame.   It
is not only an admirable picture : it has the merit of being a perfect ich-
thyological study.   The only fault, if a fault exists, is in the artist's coloring,
which is at most nothing more than a falling short of a possibly attainable
excellence.   It is deeply regretted that for several years he has almost
abandoned his easel ; for the world cannot possess so many of such pic-

tures as to make them common. He is an excellent draughtsman, and
has for some time occupied himself with pen-and-ink sketches, and the
collection of pottery and porcelain in Hartford, where he has resided
since moving from Stonington.

JOHN FERGUSON WEIR.

The professor of painting in the Yale Art School, J. F. Weir, was
born at West Point Aug. 28, 1841. He received his instruction in art
from his father. His first year of practice in New York he received two
hundred dollars for paintings, and a hundred dollars for night-work for
"The New-York Evening Post," which, with sixty dollars with which he
reached the city, more than balanced his year's expenses. It was a good
experience, and taught him where to look for success. In 1869 he went
abroad to study. This trip, however, was cut short by his accepting the
position which he now holds in New Haven. He is fond of large canvases, and has produced some popular and finely-executed pieces. His
work has been criticised as lacking in color. This seems hardly just, however, as color is evidently a secondary consideration with him. His work
is well balanced, and characteristic for truthfulness. There is no glaring
eccentricity, either in the man or his work, to leave an unpleasant impression on the mind.

JOHN S. JAMESON.

In Zion's-Hill Cemetery, at Hartford, Conn., lie the remains of John
S. Jameson, one of the many thousands sacrificed in our late war for the
Union. He was born in Hartford March 25, 1842; and died in the
Andersonville Prison Aug. 31, 1864. When only nine years old he manifested an unusual taste and ability for music, gathered from his father,
John Jameson the organist, and his mother, the celebrated singer Mrs.
Rachel S. Jameson. He also developed a talent as marked for drawing
and painting. When eleven, his parents moved with him to New York;
and during his thirteenth year he drew upon his slate a portrait so life-
like, and such an excellent likeness, that it at once attracted the attention
and admiration of several artists, chiefly Frederick E. Church, who became
the young man's fast and valuable friend, and upon his death wrote of
him, " Of all the younger artists of my acquaintance, no one has held
out better-grounded hopes of future high excellence. His standard was a
lofty one, and it appeared to me that no selfish ambition guided his hand."
In music, no less, he made rapid and astonishing progress. William
Mason, who was long an important friend, wrote, " It seemed to me I had

"THE CONFESSIONAL," BY JOHN F. WEIR.

never met a finer musical talent." The Artists' Fund Society, of which he was one of the early members, passed the following at his death, submitted by John F. Kensett, its president: —

"Had his life been spared, the rare qualities of his mind, his exquisite taste and accomplishments, and fine promise of future excellence in his art, would have reflected honor upon this society, and upon the country of his birth."

JOHN S. JAMESON.

Beyond these estimates nothing need be or could be said. Many a bright star of promise fell, shaken from its path toward a glorious zenith, by the convulsions of that bitter conflict, — probably none brighter than the promise in John S. Jameson.

HORACE WOLCOTT ROBBINS.

A member of the large family so well and widely known in Connecticut for many generations, Horace W. Robbins, the landscape-painter, was born in Mobile, Ala., Oct. 21, 1842. His father was a native of Rocky Hill, where the family came with the very first settlement. His mother was a Miss Hyde, from an equally well-known family of Norwich. He has also spent many summers sketching and painting in the State; and his wife, a Miss Phelps, is a daughter of a native of Simsbury. Altogether, the State is entitled to take a vital interest in the artist, as very closely allied to her.

Mr. Robbins received a collegiate education in Baltimore, taking the highest honors of the class. His first instruction in art was given by his father, supplemented, while pursuing his other studies, by the best teachers that could be procured. After graduating he studied with James M. Hart in New York, and, the following winter, opened a studio in that city. During the war he was a member of the famous New-York Twenty-second Regiment. He was elected a member of the Century Club in 1863, and May 10, 1864, an associate of the National Academy. In May, 1878, he was made an academician by a very flattering vote. He was made a member of the Artists' Fund in 1873, and, soon after, the secretary. In May, 1864, he sailed with F. E. Church to the Island of Jamaica, where they

HORACE WOLCOTT ROBBINS.

painted for several months. When Mr. Church returned, Mr. Robbins went at once to England. At the American Legation at Paris he was married, and passed the two succeeding winters in Paris studying art. He was fortunate in meeting and receiving instruction from Theodore Rousseau, and in visiting the studios of the leading artists of the day. The summer of 1866 he passed in sketching in Switzerland; returning to Paris for the Exposition of 1867, and to New York in the fall. Several of Mr. Robbins's largest and best pieces and many smaller sketches are from the Farmington Valley. "The Roadside Elms" and "Mount Philip" were Simsbury sketches, exhibited at the Centennial, now owned by the Attwood family of Poughkeepsie, and George F. Phelps

"ROADSIDE ELMS AT FARMINGTON," BY HORACE W. ROBBINS.

of New York. He is rapidly becoming one of the leading artists in water-color painting. He is treasurer of the Society of Painters in Water-Color, and yearly contributes productions that indicate a most promising progress. His last contribution was a view of the old Ensign House in Simsbury. This picture also appeared in the Paris Exposition of 1878.

There was a slight mannerism in Mr. Robbins's early work, which he appears to have dropped entirely within a few years, and is rapidly gaining in an independence and originality that much better become him.

NELSON A. PRIMUS.

A colored boy, Nelson A. Primus, born in Hartford 1843, was apprenticed to George Francis to learn the carriage-making and painting trade. It was a gloomy prospect, even in Hartford, and as late as 1858, to start in life with any notion of raising himself; and Nelson Primus had as hard a time as any of his race. However, with the help of Mr. Francis, who vigorously upheld him, he weathered the buffetings, and rapidly developed a strong love for art, and some ability in painting, and in 1859 received a medal from the State Agricultural Society for good drawing. He painted a trout-piece, which the scholars of the Talcott-street Sunday School purchased, and presented to the superintendent. Mr. Francis gave him some instruction. Mrs. Jerome also gave him a few lessons. Beside this, all of his studying was done by himself. In 1864 he moved to Boston, and endeavored to establish himself as a portrait-painter. He paints a very good face, and has been partially successful, but obliged to work at carriage-painting beside for support. He painted a portrait of F. J. Allen, proprietor of the Astor House, that was highly complimented by the press; and one of the actress Lizzie May Ulmer, a good likeness, and well executed.

MONTAGUE FLAGG.

The oldest son of Jared B. Flagg, grandson of Mayor Flagg, Montague, born in Hartford 1843, presents an example of talent hidden even from the possessor for many years. Finding it impossible to enter a mercantile life, he sailed to Australia. Returning, his father urged artwork upon him without success. He was twenty-six before he made his first attempt at drawing, but with such success that he at once entered upon a study of drawing. At the end of three years, developing both love for the profession and ability, he sailed for Paris, where he has since been studying under the best masters. Some time ago he sent home a portrait of the late Dr. Bushnell, which was exhibited in Hartford. It was painted in the bold French style, with many meritorious points. A small piece, "The Mysterious Text," and another, "The Young Pioneer," were exhibited in the fifty-second annual exhibition at the National Academy, eliciting much praise.

OLIN L. WARNER.

The sculptor O. L. Warner, now established in New York, was born in Suffield, Hartford County, Conn., April 9, 1844. While studying at the Seward Institute at fifteen years of age, he made several busts in chalk from engravings, with so much success, that he determined to become a sculptor. There was no way opened to him, and he studied telegraphy to supply himself with means to attempt the profession. In 1869 he went abroad, and entered the French National School of Fine Arts, where he was under Jouffroy; afterwards working in the studio of Carpeaux. He returned to America in 1872 after the Franco-Prussian war, in which, with Moller, he had joined the Foreign Legion, and been one of the best shots in the company of sharpshooters. Finding a lack of employment at first, he resolutely undertook any thing that might be brought within his line, spending all of his leisure time upon medallion heads and small ideal figures, which have proved very popular. He is a member of the Society of American Artists, and exhibited at the Philadelphia Centennial a colossal medallion of Edwin Forrest, and a bust of President Hayes at the Union League Club in 1876. A marble statue of "Night" is one of his best pieces, promising much for the possibilities before the artist.

THOMAS SEDGWICK STEELE.

T. S. Steele, born in Hartford June 11, 1845, where he has since resided, has virtually devoted his life to mercantile business, but before and after business-hours has, in the last few years, produced several paintings that entitle him to mention among Connecticut artists. A taste for outdoor sports led him into the Rangeley-Lake regions, Maine, where in 1873, to preserve the size of a six-pound trout caught with rod and line, he laid it on a piece of bark, marking the outline with a knife-blade. Within this outline he reproduced the colors of the trout with crayon. Success in this demonstrated a taste that has since led him to endeavors in oil. In the summer of 1874 his first trout-piece was favorably placed in the Brooklyn Art Academy, and in the spring of 1877 three similar paintings were hung "on the line" in the National-Academy Exhibition.   He has also been able to sell several pieces at flattering prices. Never having received any instruction, and doing much of his painting by gaslight, these are specimens of truly remarkable success, for the development of which he thanks the six-pound trout.   He is secretary and treasurer of the Hartford School of Design.

REGINALD T. SPERRY,

A son of Dr. T. S. Sperry, born in Hartford in 1845, early displayed a taste for art (which his father warmly encouraged), and received instruction in figure-painting from Alfred Hart.   When twenty-four he began a course of study in the National Academy, and, returning to Hartford, was for some time engaged in a successful art-school, in the course of which he delivered weekly lectures on art in its relations to physiology and anatomy, that were popular and instructive.   He has painted many meritorious landscapes, displaying an excellent taste for general arrangement, and a proficiency in drawing; but his forte, in which he is particularly felicitous, is offhand black-and-white designing.   In 1874 he moved from Hartford, and established himself in Brooklyn, N.Y., where he still resides. He is now preparing sketches for a series of engravings illustrative of the Connecticut Valley, from the source of the river to the Sound.

EBENEZER PLACKETT.

A young artist, E. Plackett, giving considerable promise in portrait and figure painting, settled in New Milford in 1871, where he has since remained.   He was born in Wisconsin May 24, 1844.

ERNEST SHERMAN PEASE.

A son of the engraver J. I. Pease, Ernest Sherman, born in Philadelphia November, 1846, came with his father to Salisbury, Conn., in 1872.   He paints birds and animals with much talent in water-color.   His color is especially good, taken direct from nature, of which he is evidently a faithful student.   He is a growing artist; and, if he perseveres with the same enthusiasm that has marked his course thus far, he may be sure of a popular future.

C. C. BURLEIGH, JUN.

Charles Burleigh, born in Pennsylvania 1848, was brought to Plainfield, Conn., when six months old, where his grandfather had been preceptor of the academy, and where his father was born. There he began the study of art as a portrait-painter; which branch he now pursues in Northampton, Mass.

ROBERT BOLLING BRANDEGEE.

R. B. Brandegee was born in Berlin, Conn., in April, 1849. · He possesses many of the fundamental qualities of the best artist. His love and labor for art date with his childhood. His school-day drawings are remarkable for the accuracy with which he represents the body in motion.

Fortunately, while quite young, his talent in drawing attracted the attention of a relative well able to assist the promise that was in him, giving it every facility for development. His first study was under J. Hill, the water-color artist of Nyack; after which he spent a winter under the instruction of S. C. Farrar in New York (now in London). Thus far his work had been wholly with water-color, in which he had reached a proficiency that enabled him to sell several pictures at a very good advantage. "A Study of Tulips," exhibited through the Water-Color Society, received a complimentary notice which it well deserved. His style was somewhat after his master's, but expressed withal an independence and individuality. It was fresh, strong, and vigorous. The bright sunshine and bold relief were courted in his subjects, whether with complete success or not is of comparatively little moment. They will be good qualities if held in obedience, and developed through careful education.

After attaining this degree of perfection, Mr. Brandegee returned from New York; and for two years he occupied a studio, and gave lessons to several young ladies in Hartford, — as he remarks, "with much more pleasure to himself than profit." On the 29th of April, 1872, in company with C. N. Flagg and William Faxon, jun., he sailed for Europe.

Mr. Brandegee has very sensibly put himself under a strict course of instruction, spending only vacations in making sketches in oil, of which he has sent home some interesting specimens showing most happy progress. Two of these pictures were displayed in the National-Academy Exhibition a year ago, well worthy of study, and gratifying to the friends of the artist, — "A Peasant Girl of Burgundy fishing in the Yonne," "A Peasant Woman of Cernay la Ville." For four years he studied simply drawing from casts and live models. The last year has been devoted to color and composition. A late piece, "The Wandering Musician," shows the good effects immediately resulting from this; also an excellent piece, "By the Window." "A Priest," in good color and drawing, was in the 1878 Exhibition at the National Academy, New York.

CHARLES NOEL FLAGG.

The second son of Jared B. Flagg, born in Brooklyn 1849, after studying in Paris, established himself in Hartford in 1874, where he became popular as a social, intelligent, and promising artist. In 1877, in company with D. W. Tryon, he again went to Paris, where he is still studying. A large portrait of the late Austin Dunham, sent to Hartford in January, 1877, shows much progress, a bold, free touch, and good use of color.

CHARLES E. PORTER.

The fruit-painter C. E. Porter was born in Hartford 1850. His talent for picture-making rendered him popular in the public school. When fourteen, he began a course of study in drawing; but poverty obliged him to discontinue. At sixteen he began again, and, after studying for

" STUDY OF FRUIT." — BY CHARLES E. PORTER.

two years, entered the National Academy for four terms in the antique and life schools, supporting himself by giving lessons. He then studied for a year with J. O. Easton. He has several times exhibited fine speci-

mens of his work at the National Academy.   Henry Bryant of Hartford
has been a warm friend of the artist; and, through his influence, he has
lately opened a studio in Hartford.   His fruit and flower pieces display
much talent.   They are characteristically almost without paint, the most
delicate expressions of color, faithful to nature, and very attractive.   Few
artists have obtained a better education in drawing, and few are more
deserving of success.   Being a colored man, Mr. Porter has found shame-
ful obstacles placed in his path, but is manfully fighting them with a love
of art and an enthusiasm that must conquer.

EDWIN AUGUSTUS MOORE.

A son of the landscape-painter N. A. Moore, born in Hartford Aug.
24, 1858, has taken up his father's profession with evident liking, and
already produced several specimen-pieces that do him very great credit.

"AN OWL." — BY E. A. MOORE.

D. W. TRYON.

A young artist familiarly known to many residents about Hartford,
D. W. Tryon, is now studying in Paris.   He was born in Hartford in
August, 1849.   When three years old his father died, and he was taken
by his mother to East Hartford.   When but four years old he evinced a
strong love for the pencil, and at ten, when on a trip up the Hudson,

made a sketch of an island, that created a decided enthusiasm among the passengers. Necessity compelled his entering a clerkship; but in 1871 he gave it up, and opened a studio, producing principally landscape-scenes, and giving lessons. In 1872 he married, and in 1877 sailed for Paris, where he is making a careful study of figure-painting. A landscape exhibited by him in the Kurtz Gallery, March, 1878, and later in Hartford, "Castle Elizabeth from the Sands at Jersey," is indicative of very good results from his study. Mr. Tryon possesses courage and perseverance, — two excellent qualities looking toward success in art; and great things may safely be predicted if he retain his pleasing originality.

APPENDIX.

FOLLOWING are the names of a few artists, of whom, for one cause or another, it has been impossible to learn the age, and which are consequently placed in an Appendix, having nothing to indicate their chronological position.

GEORGE BALDWIN,

A native of Thompson, Conn., born about sixty years ago, after receiving a common-school education, went to Norwich, and studied portraiture. He married in Mansfield Centre, and, after practising his art in various localities, has settled in his native place, where he is still engaged in portrait-painting.

MATTHEW WILSON.

In 1861–63 Matthew Wilson won a wide local reputation about Hartford for his life-size crayon and pastel heads, at one hundred and at fifty dollars respectively. His work possessed much spirit and grace, but was naturally somewhat unfinished through rapid execution. He often finished a head in a single day. In 1863 he removed to Brooklyn, N.Y., for a wider field of labor.

HEKKING.

Mr. Hekking, the widely-known and popular German landscape-painter, was one of the original members of the Hartford Art Association, and has practised his art through Connecticut at irregular intervals for many years.

CARL CONRADS.

Another German artist, Carl Conrads, has been for twelve years connected with the Hartford Granite Company. He is perhaps over-modest regarding his work as a sculptor, which is surely very good of its kind. Among his best designs are the figures on the Antietam Monument. In

1871 he returned to Munich for a short visit, availing himself of the opportunity for still further study. As a designer of monuments, his work stands high.

W. J. HENNESSY.

Mr. Hennessy, now in London, where he has built up a popular reputation, went there from New Haven, where he had painted for some time. Eugene Benson wrote of him in 1863, "His work indicates a sympathy for the loneliness of old age which does as much credit to his heart as the representation does to the skill of his hand." A characteristic piece, "Spring," hangs in the Yale Art Gallery. All his work seems to need is a little more of the mellowness most attractive in a picture to earn for the artist a high position.

W. ELIPHALET TERRY.

A cousin of Luther Terry the artist, W. Eliphalet Terry, spent some time in Hartford, Conn., practising art. He is especially felicitous in drawing animals, but, unfortunately fortunate financially, has lacked the encouragement of necessity to become a master. He has been remarkably successful, considering the limited attention given the subject. After studying under Luther Terry in Rome during 1846 and 1847, he spent the greater part of 1849, 1850, and 1851, in Hartford. Characteristic is a reply made to a brother-artist in that city who found him idle before a picture for several days: "I am bound I will not have two finished pictures on hand at once.

JOHN EDWARD WYLIE.

A young artist, J. E. Wylie, jun., born in New Haven, Conn., is evidently rising to a position of excellence as a water-color painter. Flower-pieces have thus far claimed his entire attention, in which he has displayed much talent. He has lately established himself in Hartford, and, with an ambition to become a figure-painter, will doubtless be prominent in the future.

ROBERT W. WISEMAN.

Several paintings of animals in the National-Academy exhibitions from the brush of Robert W. Wiseman, for the past four years established in New Haven, indicate an artist of talent. The arrangement of his work and the color is in good taste, and the modelling excellent. He promises to make a name for himself in art.

Jennie S. Loop

FEMALE ARTISTS OF CONNECTICUT.

THE question often suggests itself, why woman, who is the model, subject, centre, and soul of art, and in all that is highest and noblest in art passively, is so reluctant to become actively demonstrative. Probably it is the same spirit that urges her in every thing to refrain from becoming identified as the responsible agent; while in reality it is capable of endless demonstration, that the greatest results in the world, of comedy and tragedy, prose and poetry, fact and fancy, are of her arranging. The world over, and all time through, Mother Eve picks the apple, for good, bad, or indifferent, but is well pleased that the story should always go, "In Adam's fall we sinnèd all."

There are scores of women in Connecticut to-day who are admirable artists, but very few who are willing to be known as professionals. All honor to the few! and, if women as a class realized their powers of production as they understand their powers of persuasion, there would surely be much more boldness in the subject of art. Sketches of the few who have dared the responsibility should naturally have been placed in order with the biographical sketches preceding, but that, in deference to another peculiarity of the sex regarding age, which by some has been very strongly expressed (though by others bravely ignored), an alphabetical arrangement has been adopted, in a desire to cause no offence, while yet to make no distinction. The following thirty names form the entire list of professional female artists of whom information has been received.

MISS MARY W. BIDWELL.

An example of perseverance in overcoming many obstacles, and success in gaining a position of merit, is offered to art in Connecticut by Miss Mary Bidwell, who was born in East Hartford, in a house that for over a century had been the home of her ancestors. Her father was a farmer in the quiet town, where little thought existed for matters pertaining to the fine arts. There was no direct opposition offered to the choice of an artist's life ; but, on the other hand, there was no possible opportunity for the discovery of an artist's ambition, beyond the fact of an innate love for pictures, and a desire to copy any thing that approximated the pictorial art. The only work of art in the house was an ordinary engraving of a head ; the only pictures coming under the artist's observation those occasionally appearing in magazines and illustrated books. Her first instruction in drawing was in a few private lessons from a school-teacher who had mastered only the first principles. Following this were lectures by Miss M. A. Dwight on the use of color, delivered in Hartford in 1858. The death of Miss Dwight prevented a course of lessons that had been arranged. In 1860 lessons were engaged under George H. Durrie ; but circumstances prevented their accomplishment, and another blow was dealt upon her ambition, the more severe because her hopes and plans were secrets of her own.

At length instruction was secured under F. S. Jewett, the marine-artist, which continued for two years ; after which several months were devoted to the study of modelling clay in the Cooper Institute. Miss Bidwell still resides in East Hartford, spending her winters in Brooklyn, where her best works have been displayed in the annual exhibition of the Brooklyn Art Association.

At the first annual exhibition of the Hartford Art Association Miss Bidwell was represented by an excellent medallion "Head of Christ," one of her few works in clay, and a "Portrait Bust," beside several oil-paintings, which were commented upon by critics at the time as possessing a merit and worth not often obtained by female artists in America. Her style is free, her coloring upon landscapes faithful to nature. She has sketched continually in the open air, making several trips to the Adirondacks, returning with studies displaying a decided artistic ability, the more remarkable for the circumstances under which it was nourished.

MRS. ALICE HART BIDWELL.

Miss Alice Hart, now the wife of Dr. J. W. Bidwell of Winsted, has painted many pictures worthy of notice. She was born in Barkhamsted. When very young, evidently possessing the qualifications prominently desirable in the artist, she fortunately found herself in circumstances offering little or no opposition. At fourteen years old she began a course of instruction under F. S. Jewett. She was his first pupil, and naturally received a good degree of attention and assistance, under which she progressed rapidly, and for ten years occupied a studio with Miss Mary Bidwell in Hungerford & Cone's block, Hartford. Marriage had the natural effect of limiting the hours before the easel. Soon another and even more potent obstacle was placed in the way of further progress in the appearance of a trouble with the eyes, which finally caused her to abandon art entirely. Mrs. Dr. Bidwell has, however, ample consolation for her own sacrifice in the shape of a daughter five years old, already passionately bound to her pencil and paper, giving pleasing hope for a brilliant future.

MISS FLORA CATLIN,

A sister of Ex-Gov. Julius Catlin of Hartford, born in Litchfield, Conn., moved to Hartford on the death of her father in 1829. She resided with her brother, and, having obtained an excellent education in the rudiments of art, for the occupation of leisure hours devoted them to instructing large classes in the Hartford Female Seminary under Mr. Brace and Miss Beecher, in which capacity she exerted her influence for art in the State, which has appeared in force in later lives. Miss Catlin at present resides in Boston.

MISS SARAH B. GILBERT.

Some fine pottery and porcelain decorations and flower-pieces come from Miss Gilbert's studio in New Haven. The artist has also attempted several figure-pieces, but without such marked success. Among the latter was an interesting piece displayed at the first exhibition in the New-Haven Art Building. The design was peculiar. A lady, on steamer-deck, sat with her back to the foreground, looking seaward. It was well executed. Miss Gilbert was an ardent student in the Cooper Institute.

MISS CARRIE GRISWOLD,

A young artist promising much for the future, who was born in Hartford, studied under Mrs. Jerome of Hartford, and Leutze in New York. She was a skilful copyist, and beginning to produce meritorious original work, when she died, at the very outset of her career, in Florida, whither she had gone for her health.

MISS ANNE HALL.

In the hereditary passage of art-love and æsthetic sympathy from father to child, and child to grandchild, Miss Anne Hall, third daughter of the late and celebrated Dr. Jonathan Hall of Pomfret, Conn., came into possession of an ardent love for every thing pertaining to the fine arts. Her father had crushed the feeling in his own breast on account of an apparent necessity to turn his attention another way. He followed his father through the medical profession; but when his daughter appeared, promising the same love, he eagerly fostered it in her, giving her every possible advantage of materials and copies to test the depth of her ardor. Under this favorable sky she indulged her fondness for art to the extent of copying many pictures, and painting birds and flowers in water-color. These pictures proved so successful, that other friends were enlisted; and, when upon a short visit in Newport, she received instruction of Seth King, a former teacher of Allston. Later she moved to New York, where a brother resided, and began a course of study in miniature-painting on ivory and porcelain. She copied many large pictures in miniature with remarkable success; and was unanimously elected an academician, the only lady executive in the society. Two of her copies of Guido are especially noteworthy for their delicate coloring. "A Greek Girl," an original, won her the academy election. An interesting incident, indicative of the spirit of the lady, is related by Gen. Cummings in his "Annals of the National Academy." Mr. Inman was dying. It was agreed among the executive members of the academy to pass resolutions that should insure a helping hand for the families of artists after their death. This was especially arranged with a view to Mr. Inman's condition. It was necessary that it should be passed before his death, which was imminent. Gen. Cummings had done every thing in his power; but artists as a class, though the most ready of men to will a helping hand, procrastinate. A quorum could not be gathered. Miss Hall had never cast a vote; but Mr. Cummings, determined upon a despairing effort, induced her to promise, that, if on the appointed night he could not do without her, she would exercise her right. The night came, and every exertion failed. Miss Hall was sent for, and appeared. Still they lacked one. They adjourned to the dying man's chamber, and there, while they supported him, read the resolution; and he cast his last vote as Miss Hall cast her *only* vote. It was a brave, true-hearted action, denoting a brave, true-hearted artist.

The painting of "A Greek Girl" has been engraved; and several of her original miniature-paintings have received the rare and extreme compliment of being copied in enamel in France, and hence made indestructible. In New York she studied miniature-painting under A. Robertson. Her work is remarkable for its accuracy in likeness and modelling, and characteristic in delicate coloring. Miniature groups often returned her five hundred dollars each.

"AFTER THE WAR." FROM A PAINTING YET UNFINISHED.
BY MRS. JEROME.

MRS. ELIZABETH GILBERT JEROME.

Mrs. Jerome, one of the female artists on whom Connecticut has good cause to pride herself, was born in New Haven. She very early evinced a desire to look into art, but was forbidden the liberty of drawing at home. She filled her copy-books at school with works that attracted the attention of her teacher, who, seeing her evident talent, began giving her lessons after school. This was discovered by a step-mother; and at the age of fifteen all the drawings she had collected were destroyed, and a final stop put upon any thing of the sort in the future. Not until she was twenty-seven years old was an opportunity offered for her to take another step toward the goal she longed to approach. Then, coming to Hartford, she began the study of drawing under Professor Busch. He was delighted with her work, and insisted upon her going to New York and taking lessons there. She entered the Springley Institute, and at the same time spent much of her leisure in studying the work of masters that came within her reach, examining their methods, selecting their individual charms, and endeavoring to imitate them in original designs, resorting to nature for freshness and inspiration. When thirty, she returned to Hartford; since which time she has remained in that city, with the exception of a single winter, when she studied from cast and life in the National Academy, and color under E. Leutze. During this winter she painted in Mr. Leutze's studio a half-orange so successfully, that he advised a picture with it for the centre. He exhibited the picture when finished, and sold it for nearly enough to pay the artist's expenses for the winter.

Mrs. Jerome was married when thirty-two, and has necessarily carried on her art under some difficulties since then, but has not deserted it. She exhibited for the first time in the National Academy in 1866. She paints portraits with success, and, with her superior education in art, is able to give most satisfactory instruction to pupils. Ideal figure-painting is the branch in which she chiefly excels, combining with a refined taste a good eye for color, excellent modelling, and power of imparting thought and action harmoniously and expressively. Her work occupies a high position in that of the female artists of America.

MRS. MARY ANN JOHNSON.

Miss Mary Douglas, afterward the wife of the Hon. John Johnson, cannot well be omitted from Connecticut art. By some strange combination of circumstances, she did not discover her ability till four years after her marriage, but from that time applied herself with such zeal, that before her death, which came very early, she had reaped a good harvest of praise, and derived a flattering income. She was markedly successful in still-life. Several of her pictures are now owned in New London, where she painted them, evincing care and a refined taste.

MISS ABBY TRUMBULL LANMAN.

Col. Trumbull's favorite niece, Miss Lanman of Norwich, has gathered up a part of the great artist's mantle. She has shunned gaining a name of public repute, but has produced many fruit and flower pieces of great merit.

MISS SARAH LEFFINGWELL.

Some very pretty flower-pieces have been produced by Miss Sarah Leffingwell of Colchester. Ill health prevents the accomplishment of any thing at present.

MRS. HENRY A. LOOP.

A sister of Judge Lynde Harrison, the celebrated portrait and figure painter, Mrs. Loop, was born in New Haven, Conn. A line of noble ancestors instilled a blood that must have made a bold mark somewhere; and it is fortunate for art that the attention of their descendant was turned in that direction. The governors Roger and Oliver Wolcott; the first pastor of New Haven, and the first pastor of Branford; Nathaniel Lynde, one of the first settlers of Saybrook; the first pastor of Madison, and the Hon. Thomas Harrison, — are all of the ancestral line. When seventeen, the artist commenced her study in drawing under Professor Louis Bail, practising crayon-drawing from life at home. When twenty, she began the study of oil portrait-painting under Wales Hotchkiss, and also took a few lessons of George Durrie of New Haven. She then opened a studio as a professional portrait-painter. In her study and profession she has invariably painted from life, resulting in the exquisite color and living flesh-tints which her figures possess, and the freedom and originality of her portraits. In 1863 she went to New York to study Couture's method from his pupil Henry A. Loop. The successful teacher became the successful suitor; since which date Mrs. Loop has resided in New York, excepting the time occupied in a trip through Europe, studying the galleries, but, in accordance with the rule of her early life, copying nothing.

In 1875 Mrs. Loop was made an associate of the National Academy, and in 1876 came within one vote of being elected an academician. Portrait-painting has been her forte; but some fine ideal pieces have also been

"A BOQUET FOR MAMA." BY MRS. H. A. LOOP.

produced on her easel. She has adopted to some extent the style of Couture, adding the warmth and freshness to her popular portraits of women and children. There has been manifestly great improvement in her work in the past few years, and many critics have granted her a position at the head of the female figure-painters of America. Elaborate execution, enhanced by a charming simplicity, renders her pictures invariably attractive. "The Little Runaway," an Academy picture, is thoroughly characteristic. Childhood's mischief, joy, health, strength, carelessness, and hope are wonderfully united in a little half-naked wanderer, who, having run away from home, is lying down in the grass to rest, and contemplate the situation.

MISS A. E. MARSH.

Miss Marsh, a native of Nottingham, N.H., has for many years practised the profession principally as a landscape-painter in Hartford. She was one of the original members of the Hartford Art Association. Within a few years she has given up her studio, being in delicate health.

MISS CHARLOTTE ELLEN McLEAN.

A young artist just now coming very favorably before the public, Miss C. E. McLean, was born and still resides in South Glastonbury, Conn. She paints in both oil and water color, chiefly the latter; and has had on exhibition some very pretty flower-pieces. She took lessons of Mr. Tryon before he left for Europe.

MISS IRENE E. PARMELY.

In 1872 an aspirant to an artist's life, Miss I. E. Parmely, began the study of drawing under Henry Bryant of Hartford. In 1873 she went to New Haven, and there took lessons for a year under Nathaniel Jocelyn, and for a year in the Yale Art Building. In 1875 she removed to Springfield, where she has opened a studio as a professional artist, though she writes that she is only a student. There is promise of power, which the future must unfold.

MISS ELLEN M. POMEROY.

For several years Miss E. M. Pomeroy has been established in Hartford, her native city. Never fully recovering from an attack of scarlet-fever, the artist as a child held herself aloof from other children, and almost involuntarily drifted into a life of art. She studied drawing under Seth Cheney, and in 1863 began lessons in portrait-painting in oil with Mr. W. R. Wheeler. Though portraiture is her profession, she has arranged some very attractive pieces of fruit and flowers. Her work is quiet, but carefully executed, and possesses many meritorious qualities. She is at present renewing study in London.

MRS. S. C. PORTER.

A native of Hartford, Mrs. S. C. Porter, studied drawing under Mr. Gladwin and Seth Cheney in 1857 and 1858. In 1859 she engaged in a course of study in New York, and in 1863 took lessons in oil-painting for a year under Mr. Wheeler of Hartford. In 1873 Mrs. Porter went abroad, and studied for a year from casts in Paris. A great improvement in touch

"STUDY OF A HEAD."—BY MRS. PORTER.

and finish was made during this study, evidenced in the head of a girl which she painted toward the close of the year. It is executed with much skill, boldly and effectively painted, and evidently very true to life. It was one of the favored paintings in the Paris *salon* of 1875, and exhibited at the Centennial Exhibition in Philadelphia. It is the bust portrait of a poor girl taken from the streets of Paris, remarkably well modelled. The work is throughout expressive of a skilled hand, and has reflected much credit upon the artist.

MRS. LYDIA JANE PIERSON.

Miss L. J. Wheeler, an aunt of the portrait-painter W. R. Wheeler, born in Middletown, Conn., was among the pioneers of her sex in art in the State. As a child she evinced a passionate love of the beautiful, expressing it in both painting and poetry. In each she was self-taught; in both she was simple, natural, and talented. When fourteen years old, her parents moved to New-York State; and at an early age she married, and went as a farmer's wife into the then thoroughly wild district of Northern Pennsylvania, to a home twenty miles from any village. Uninspiring as the surroundings were, her poetry yet brought her popularly before the world. One spirited poem, read during a discussion in the State legislature, secured for the author, who was then in almost destitute circumstances, the gift of a snug farm from a prominent politician. She painted in water-color, chiefly selecting fruit or flowers, boldly, easily, and in excellent color. She died leaving a work unfinished that would have proved a novel and interesting combination of nature, pen, and pencil. She was preparing a volume of colored engravings of every flower of America, with a descriptive poem for each. The flowers were already prepared for the engraver at the time of her death.

MISSES SARA J. AND ESTHER L. SMITH.

Among those female artists who directly and indirectly are doing much for art in Connecticut to-day appear the names of the Misses Smith. Connecticut born and bred, through childhood and youth ardent lovers of the beautiful in nature, they formed the idea in 1869 of making art, in which they had already received an education, a life profession. Since then it has been an absorbing occupation. In 1870 they moved to Greenfield, Mass., where the eldest sister gave instruction in drawing in the public schools, which she has since continued in Hartford with marked success and popularity. Aside from her school-work in Greenfield, she instructed a large evening class. Her ambition has been toward oil-painting, and she has executed some attractive figure-pieces; but delicate health has prohibited long confinement before the easel.

Her sister, Miss Esther L. Smith, has continued the profession of a portrait-painter, for which she first received instruction of Edwin White in New York. Since moving to Hartford she has been fully occupied with orders, and there and elsewhere has painted many well-known characters ; among them Theodore D. Judah, Col. G. T. Davis, Rev. Mr. Sabire, Supreme-Court Judge T. B. Butler, a son of George Francis Train, and many others, making a specialty of children, and obtaining good likenesses.

MRS. LILY LYMAN STOCKING.

Miss L. Lyman was born in Hartford, where she studied painting in both oil and water color, and had obtained considerable excellence in small fruit and flower pieces, when she married, and moved to Detroit.

MISS MARY ADELINE TIFFANY.

Among the successful *genre*-painters of Connecticut to-day is Miss M. A. Tiffany, born and now residing in Hartford. Naturally inclined toward the close companions music and painting, she has carried both to a degree of pleasing excellence. Her first lessons in drawing were given by her sister : afterward she studied under Professors Bail and Alvergnat in outline and crayon. When sixteen she began copying flowers from nature, and at nineteen work in oil under direction of Henry Bryant, and freehand-drawing under Professor Gladwin, now in Worcester. In 1869 she accepted a position as drawing and music teacher in the Natchaug School, Willimantic ; whence, after two years, she went to Springfield, and gathered about her a large class of ladies and children. In 1873 she returned to Hartford, and for two years studied water-color painting with Mr. Tryon, at the same time drawing from casts in the Connecticut School of Design. In accordance with the fashion and the time, she has very successfully undertaken the decoration of mats, silk, and pottery, with original designs. Few artists obtain a more complete education. The result must be gratifying and satisfactory. Naturally she has become an excellent draughtsman ; and her work in both oil and water color, including several landscapes, displays much talent, accuracy, and good taste. A " Study of Chickens," in the Centennial Loan Exhibition at Hartford, elicited much praise.

THE MISSES WARD.

Two ladies, at present connected with the Decorative Art Society of New York, for several years taught drawing and decorative painting in Guilford, Conn. Miss Hattie L. H. Ward paints flowers in water-color in a bold, effective fashion ; and her sister, Miss Susan Ward, decidedly excels in the popular art of decorating pottery.

MRS. LILY GILLETT WARNER,

A daughter of the Hon. Francis Gillett of Hartford, where she was born and still resides, from an ardent love for art has developed an unusual talent in painting remarkably sweet flower-pieces. She lately wrote and illustrated for "St. Nicholas" a poem that won for her flattering commendation. Not so thoroughly a professional artist as one might wish on examining the excellence of her work, she has yet given to the public much that merits a position in Connecticut's art.

MRS. WASHBURN AND MRS. BADGE,

Two daughters of George Munger of New Haven, inheriting their father's talent, and studying under him, possess a skill that for the sake of art might profitably have been brought into much more active publicity than has been the case. Mrs. Badge has prepared and illustrated a volume of flowers that by able critics is pronounced the best work of the sort ever issued in America, while her sister has produced a few very delicate and acceptable miniature-portraits on ivory.

MISS MINNIE WATSON.

Some charming work in still-life has lately appeared from the easel of Miss Minnie Watson of East Windsor. She was a pupil of D. W. Tryon in Hartford in 1875, and is now studying in New York. Her work appears carefully true, the color especially commendable. She has this summer (1878) accepted a position which will cause her removal to Saratoga.

MRS. MARY WESTON.

The romantic history of the daughter of the poor but rigid Presbyterian minister in the desolate town of Hebron, N.H., is too well known for repetition. After painting flowers and faces in colors manufactured from leaves, beet-juice, &c., and twice running away from home in search of any one who could teach her something, she reached Hartford with but ten dollars and a bundle of clothes, and was taken into the home of the Rev. Henry Jackson. After several months of study and miniature-painting, that gave her, with the generosity of her friends, a sufficient income to live upon, she accepted an invitation to go to Willington to paint Squire Rider's family, and, as it transpired, several others for five dollars each, the sitters furnishing the ivory, while she ground her own colors.

After returning to Mr. Jackson, she fell, unfortunately for art, into the happy coils of matrimony, and virtually gave up the art of painting for the art of making a beautiful home for Mr. Weston of New York. The "Angel Gabriel" and "Infant Saviour" are her masterpieces, the flesh-tints in which are remarkably fine.

MISS E. WOOD.

An artist in East Windsor, Conn., Miss E. Wood, has won merited praise for some choice panel-pictures of birds, skilfully wrought, well drawn, and in good color. She has also produced attractive flower-pieces.